FORMATIVE THEOLOGICAL EDUCATION

FORMATIVE THEOLOGICAL EDUCATION

EDITED BY

COLLEEN M. GRIFFITH AND HOSFFMAN OSPINO

Paulist Press
New York / Mahwah, NJ

Cover design by Joe Gallagher
Book design by Lynn Else

Library of Congress Data Control Number: 2023934287

ISBN 978-0-8091-5641-2 (paperback)
ISBN 978-0-8091-8804-8 (e-book)

Published by Paulist Press
997 Macarthur Boulevard
Mahwah, New Jersey 07430
www.paulistpress.com

Printed and bound in the
United States of America

In gratitude for Dean Thomas Stegman, SJ,
whose formative leadership inspired a faculty to
reach for excellence in theological education

CONTENTS

PREFACE

Colleen M. Griffith and Hosffman Ospino

THERE IS SOMETHING significant happening in theological education today. It no longer is being done from the towering heights it once had, and this is a rich blessing. And its tendency to tilt dominantly toward the rational, toward abstract reasoning for the sake of cognitive knowing alone in matters of faith, has lost its lure. In our time, theological education aims to reclaim a richly formative purpose, that of discerning, articulating, and urging lived ways of Christian faith in the world in response to the gospel and the invitation of the Spirit. This is a purpose in keeping with a biblical way of knowing that encompasses full person engagement, contemplative attending, and meaningful personal and communal agency. As theological education continues to deepen in this more formative direction, it will step off any pedestals that remove it from the life of the world and will set its sight squarely on ethical and transformative engagement in history.

The language "formative education" has come to signal a host of liberating actions and sensibilities. It indicates the keeping of whole persons and contexts in view in teaching/learning endeavors, along with cultivation of a relational understanding of persons and a forging of communities of belonging. Formative education places emphasis on content choices that engage both intellect and affect and that foster imagination and hope. In a distinctly theological ambit, formative education espouses acting justly, loving compassionately, and walking humbly with God (see Mic 6:8), all of which require attentiveness and discernment with respect to concrete matters presenting themselves in the throes of specific times and places.

Recognizing formative education as an approach to teaching in which such aims are prized, this book reaches out to *theological educators* in a direct way. It provides access to some of the key commitments and practices of *formative education*, a term embraced by our authors as a richly textured spiritual vision. The text itself is divided into three parts. The first section offers essential grounding for emerging discussions of formative theological education. The second identifies foundational commitments of teaching theology with formative intent. And the third articulates a set of hopes that one group of formative theological educators holds for this distinctive approach in the work they do.

For several years now, Boston College's School of Theology and Ministry has been at the helm in discussions regarding the fundamental building blocks of formative theological education. In these discussions, we have sought to be attentive, reflective, and agential in developing what we believe to be a fruitful approach to teaching theology, something that can encourage spiritual maturity, ethically responsible lives, and leadership in the pursuit of justice. Our book brings together the voices of ten prominent scholars who have been part of these discussions and who demonstrate excellence themselves as formative theological educators, as evidenced in their teaching, ways of mentoring, and publications. The insights and suggestions they offer are both theoretically rich and deeply practical. They are also timely. Ours is a historical moment ripe for advancing a way of doing Christian theological education for "the life of the world" (John 6:51).

In a lingering COVID-19 ethos, in which there has been both a painfully palpable languishing of spirits and evidence of widespread divisions and disparities, theological educators, like many in leadership, question the efficacy of their work and the nature and purpose of what they do. One strong intent of this book is to renew the confidence of disheartened educators by bringing a vision of formative theological education into full focus. A strengthening in this way of educating is urged, and to this end, an array of practical pedagogical strategies is offered that can be utilized in teaching.

As contributing editors, we hope that this book will invite fresh conversations among theological educators at every level and within multiple contexts. We remain confident that such dialogue calls all of us to a rekindled embrace of theological education as a noble art that, when coupled with God's generous grace, holds the potential to shape mindsets, footsteps, and hearts in ways that indeed contribute to a more just and compassionate church, nation, and world.

ACKNOWLEDGMENTS

AS COEDITORS, we are grateful for the original essays contributed by our colleagues for this volume. Our authors, well-established scholars in their fields, bring unique and substantive perspectives to a contemporary discussion of formative education, and they do so specifically as theological educators who are passionate about what they do and highly successful in the classroom. We are thankful for their care for the project and their commitment to the collegial process that has led to this book.

We wish to acknowledge a group of Boston College doctoral students in theology and education who participated in a focus group with some of our authors early on in the process to discuss their hopes for formative theological education. We extend our thanks to Cesar "CJ" Baldelomar, Diane Francesca Oliveros, Hannah Sutton-Adams, and Raphael Augustine Yabut for their involvement in this discussion. And we wish to recognize the outstanding contribution of Mary O'Shan Overton, PhD, Director of the Center for Writing and Learning Support and Faculty Mentor for the DMin Program in Creative Writing and Public Theology at Pittsburgh Theological Seminary, for her careful attention to detail in copyediting all of the essays.

We greatly appreciate the initial grant we received for this project from Boston College's Office of the Provost that provided material support and enabled all ten authors to gather for a full day at Boston College's Connors Center for a lively exchange of ideas having read one another's essays in early draft form.

Finally, we are especially grateful to Donna M. Crilly and the entire team at Paulist Press for their support of this work.

Colleen M. Griffith and Hosffman Ospino

Part One

GROUNDING THE DISCUSSION

1

FORMATIVE EDUCATION

Bringing A Vision into Focus

Colleen M. Griffith

HOW DOES ONE reflect on an enigmatic term like *formative education* keeping multiple strands of thought in view? Mind mapping is a focusing tool, one that prompts people to be more conscious of the connections and associations they carry in response to a designated word or phrase. This effective form of visual brainstorming has been used by noteworthy thinkers and artists like Leonardo da Vinci and Pablo Picasso, and it is something that can be adopted by anyone seeking to think about a core concept in an expansive way that generates insight.

One begins to mind-map by placing a key word or phrase of interest at the center of one's page. Moving centrifugally then, using line, color, and shape, one creates sprays or branches that spill outward in numerous directions. The branches map sub-ideas, appropriation points, explications, and expansions of the key word or phrase at the center. The focal idea assumes proportions as though taking on flesh, resulting in a fuller grasp of it for the creator of the mind map and for those engaged visually with it.

When formative education serves as the foundational concept in a mind mapping exercise, connecting thoughts and associations stretch out like sinews and tendons, giving bodily shape to this notion. *Formative education... "keeps the whole person in view," "cares about development of character," "values appropriation of one's learning," "fosters inclusive communities," "cultivates a relational sense of the human," "is interested in meaning and purpose," "raises hopes," "attends to content intellectually and affectively," "encourages openness and dialogue," "welcomes contextual standpoints," "expands the self," "advances creativity," and "connects learning and the world."* Promising avenues for exploration surface as subsets of association rise to the fore. Considered as a whole, the many offshoots testify to much of what is gripping about "formative education."

As formative education sheds its abstraction for fleshly proportions, a compelling vision comes into view. This vision is notably spiritual in its concern for *whole persons* and its understanding of the task of integration unique to each. The vision is also spiritual both in its hope for the *practical relevance of learning* in relation to the world and its active desire for *inclusive communities of belonging* in which interdependence is prized. This threefold vision of formative education claims the attention of this chapter.[1] The chapter is mindful that a "line of sight" emerges here for theological educators, one that has the capacity to inspire one's teaching anew with practical effect. And this "line of sight" resonates deeply with points of emphasis found in the historic Christian spiritual tradition.

A Vision of the Person in the Learning Process

Formative education suggests more than mere communication of information to interested seekers. It hopes for more, models more, intends something greater. This way of educating highlights the importance of teachers becoming adept at directing attention to the whole persons of their students and their contexts. Students are socioculturally situated. They have aspirations and distinct questions, and they come into a learning environment at differing points of development, each with their own path of becoming. Every member of any learning community is embodied, embedded, emergent, relational, and unique. Practitioners of a formative way of education grasp this and value it. They are ready to listen to the concerns and hopes of diverse students in their teaching and eager to help students cultivate their respective abilities to reflect, discern, and come to know for themselves.

Theological educators will find the historic Christian spiritual tradition to be a most helpful resource for underscoring this outreach to the whole person, and the work of integration unique to each, in the Ignatian-based principle *cura personalis*. The Latin *cura personalis* signals "care for the person," something viewed in Ignatian spirituality to be essential in both spiritual direction and education. Though not a phrase used directly by Ignatius himself, *cura personalis* has traceable roots in Ignatius's *Spiritual Exercises* and teachings.[2] Ignatius of Loyola (1491–1556) exhibited strong concern for the physical and emotional well-being of retreatants and students and brought keen awareness to the emerging movements of the Spirit that were particular to each person.

Cura personalis as an actual term was used first and systematized by the Jesuit Wlodimer Ledóchowski, Superior General of the Society of Jesus from 1915–1942; he coined it to refer to the care necessary to foster students' "moral, spiritual and intellectual development."[3] In 1972, over thirty years later, Superior General Pedro Arrupe spoke of *cura personalis* as "the concern, care, attention, even love of the teacher for each student—in an atmosphere of deep personal trust."[4] The Dutch Jesuit Peter Hans Kolvenbach, Superior General of the Society of Jesus from 1983–2008, wrote about *cura personalis* as "a constitutive element in Jesuit education and formation,"[5] describing it as "help, from person to person, so that God and (the human) may really meet."[6]

Jesuit historian Barton T. Geger highlights three meanings of this Ignatian-influenced referent found in Jesuit mission and school documents.[7] The first is that of a holistic education that attends to all dimensions of personhood and not simply to intellectual development. The second points to education that is mindful of the particular needs and identity of each learner. And the third underscores the responsibility of administrators and leaders to show attentiveness and concern for persons working in their institutions. All three meanings, in the assessment of Geger, are "consonant with the values and practical experience of Ignatius."[8]

These operative senses of *cura personalis* identified by Geger provide guidance to educators and administrators seeking to teach and lead in formative ways. The first offers a corrective to perceptions of teaching as being about an imparting of information only, typical of a banking model of education.[9] The second reminds those who teach that the distinctiveness of persons means one size never fits all and that creation of personalized pedagogy is an important aspect of care for the uniqueness of persons. The third sense steers in a communal direction; *cura personalis*, something typically construed in individualized interpersonal terms, signals something for the policies and procedures of institutions as well. Developing this point, Julia Bninski and Jennifer Wozniak Boyle observe: "Theorizing *cura personalis* as an institutional practice avoids the kind of limited moral imagination that can only envision 'the good' as a matter of individual choices or individual responsibilities."[10] *Cura personalis* provides a grounding for the construction of holistic institutional support systems for learning communities and for the fostering of work environments that enable faculty to accompany and mentor students well.

For theological educators drawn to this notion of *cura personalis*, staying present to the movements of students in their distinctiveness as they journey toward increased levels of learning and integration becomes a desired end-view. Doing so requires consciousness of the real circumstances that students face in order to invite discernment and growth effectively within live contexts. Trusted relationship between teachers and students sprouts when this happens, impacting the felt sense of the learning community for all involved, which, in turn, begins to influence students' responsiveness to one another.

The American educational philosopher Nel Noddings identifies *presence* as a vital aspect of "care."[11] Presence involves more than feeling passion for one's subject matter; it means being passionate about the human beings involved in the learning process as well. Educational institutions sometimes construe teaching "as a checklist of behaviors, dispositions, measures, and standards," short shrifting altogether the "presence" of the educator. And what is "presence?" Carol Rodgers and Miriam Raider-Roth define it as "a state of alert awareness, receptivity, and connectedness to the mental, emotional, and physical workings of both the individual and the group in the context of their learning environments."[12] Rodgers and Raider-Roth add that it also includes "the ability to respond with a considered and compassionate best next step"[13] in learning situations.

For theological educators, "presence" entails bringing one's whole self to attend to what is happening in the moment and perceiving its import well with the help of the Spirit. The Latin root of "attend," *attendere*, means to stretch toward, and the Latin root of "perceive," *percipere*, implies a becoming more wholly aware in one's senses.[14] In acts of attending and perceiving, the self of the educator is always expanded as connections to others and to a larger world increase. As for students, exposure to a teacher who communicates "presence" enables them to feel recognized, encouraging a greater degree of openness to new ways of thinking and being.

In short, *cura personalis* is a way of care for the full person that kindles growth and becoming. When students experience it over time, they are more likely to model this way of response in relation to others they encounter. Thus, demonstration and reception of this way of care contributes to the formation of people more capable of solidarity with others.

A Vision of the Practical Relevance of Learning

The spiritual vision to which the notion of formative education gives rise includes concern for the multidimensional development of persons, and it also carries hope for the practical relevance of learning in relation to a wider world full of concrete historical challenges and needs. Theological educators seeking to resource students in ways of knowing that help them to address more adequately the pressing questions and concerns of their time will want to invite an engagement in the world that stays conscious of the love and largesse of God as their lead. Theological educators can help students "to discern, articulate, and commend visions of flourishing life in light of God's self-revelation in Christ"[15] and to do this in particular times and places.

Never an isolated discipline carried out in a vacuum, theological education takes place amidst concrete situations. At its best, it will provide access to the wisdom of the Christian tradition and the God of love revealed in Jesus Christ that stands at the center of it. This way of educating aims to foster discernment of the impulse of the Spirit in the concretely real, and to offer tools for living in and living out one's Christian faith in the world. The content of theological education therefore becomes necessarily dynamic rather than static. And it holds the potential to invite what M. Shawn Copeland identifies as "practical theological agency" in the world.[16]

Theological educators committed to the practical relevance of learning, who value appropriation of one's knowing in acts of engagement in the world, will find historical resonance and a source of inspiration in the Salesian spiritual tradition, with its emphasis on knowledge and love of God being exercised practically in the world. The exercise of love of God is, in the words of Francis de Sales, to be "affective and effective,"[17] something that unites the heart of God and the heart of the human, creating "an affinity" through which persons are joined to God's goodness for the sake of becoming manifestations of God's ways in concrete actual circumstances. The union of the human spirit with God then not only brings persons to new knowing of God but into "loving society with our neighbors."[18]

Francis de Sales (1567–1622) and Jane Frances de Chantal (1572–1641) were spiritual figures whose way of living the Christian life and spiritually guiding others became known as the Salesian way. Together they envisioned and formed the Congregation of the Visitation in 1610, a unique women's congregation forged in response to the desires of women like Jane herself to practice Christian life in intentional community specifically as widows, women with children, women with disabilities, and women who were too old or weak to opt for a traditional religious life. Francis and Jane took up the task of the spiritual revitalization of their society, and both regularly wrote letters of spiritual direction that were passed down and preserved as part of the treasury of the Christian spiritual tradition. The two enjoyed a strong spiritual friendship over the course of their lives, coming to know friendship rooted in God as a grace-filled gift, something they wrote about often and exemplified.

Their common message was one of realizing the love of God in the world and doing so with gentle regard and reverence for that action of God. Francis and Jane emphasized God's way of calling persons at all social levels and from every profession into the depths of love of God in Christ. They sensed this love to be exercised and appropriated in lifestyles as multiple as society offered. Convinced that, by sheer dint of the goodness enacted in any given person's life context, others would be invited to enter into the Source of all love, the two remained confident that life lived under the guidance and initiative of the Spirit and formed by the values of Christ was both conceivable and a worthy aspiration.

Grounding this confidence was an understanding of God as love inclined toward the human, and of the human as having a natural capacity to incline toward God as well. This was imaged in Salesian spirituality as Divine-human "mutual breathing and beating of hearts."[19] Speaking of God in the activity of prayer, Francis de Sales writes, "We aspire to God and breathe in God, and God reciprocally inspires us and breathes upon us."[20] Though worldly evidence of the human not being in sync with the Divine breath and heart certainly abounded, Francis and Jane stood resolute in their conviction that it was possible, through Christ, "to breathe in concert with divine affectivity"[21] and thereby to advance the Christ reality in the world.

The Salesian motto "Live Jesus" written at the start of all their letters underscored this hope; this mantra continues to serve many to this day. "Thank God, Who has made you for so gracious an end,"[22] exclaims Francis in response to this profound human calling in the *Introduction to the Devout Life*. The presentation of Jesus envisioned and advanced by Francis and Jane was one of gentleness and expansiveness of heart; Salesian spirituality historically has claimed that gentleness, which carries the implication of nonviolence, challenges the world, and that continual growth in the relational virtues of gentleness, patience, and humility, reflective of the heart of Jesus, prove powerful practices of testimony in the world.[23]

Christian theological educators do well to place hope in the transformation of the human heart into the heart of Jesus for the sake of the world, making this goal focal to their teaching. Embracing such a vision, indeed knowing one's desire for it for oneself and for one's students, undoubtedly can guide content choices and strategies for appropriation in teaching practice. This too, however, warrants a gentle approach. Theological educators benefit from heeding the advice of Jane de Chantal offered in a letter of spiritual direction written to her brother, Andre Fremyot, Archbishop of Bourges: "Perform your actions calmly and gently, and keep your mind ever joyful, peaceful and content. Do not worry about your perfection or your soul. God to whom it belongs will take care of it and fill it with all the graces, consolations, and blessings of God's holy love in the measure that they will be useful in this life."[24] Influenced by a Salesian aesthetic, the relational values of Jesus's heart can exert positive influence within communities of theological education.

A Vision of Generative Communities of Belonging

Visions inspire and they challenge. The vision of communities of inclusion and belonging reflected in formative education pushes theological educators to consider many things: What understanding of Christian community am I educating toward, and what does this mean for my modeling of the learning community itself? How is community fashioned so that it becomes a healthy, safe space where belonging gets fostered? What is it that makes a community hospitable, expansive, and abundant in compassionate regard?

Writing about the value of generative interdependence[25] in community, Sharon D. Welch observes: "We are called to be bold. We are called to take risks. We are called to resist and build on our strengths in responsible and creative ways."[26] These calls so often are invitations of the Spirit, and courageous human response is more likely when there is experience of and participation in a steadying "beloved community of belonging." For Willie James Jennings, the theologian who coined this rich phrase, "belonging must become the hermeneutical starting point from which we think the social, the political, the individual, the ecclesial, and most crucial for this work, the educational."[27] Jennings presses forward with a mandate: "Theological education must capture its central work—to form...in the art of cultivating belonging."[28]

The cultivation of belonging will not be foregrounded if persons operate with a declaration-of-independence mentality. Strong valuation of autonomy and self-sufficiency has influenced choices of pedagogical practice often resulting in a privileging of individualist, privatistic, and primarily independent ways of learning. But, as Sharon Welch notes, declarations of independence are never enough.[29] Strength lies in the ever stouter and more profound declarations of *interdependence* to which we commit ourselves, and in the shaping of learning communities founded on this declaration. A community that knows the value of "generative interdependence" will be one that "values diversity and connection, that nurtures creativity and scientific rigor, that embodies responsibility for others and the freedom to find new and better ways of living out, and creating, expansive communities of connection, respect and cooperation."[30] Generosity toward the other, toward the raw places in oneself, toward the stranger, and toward those beyond the boundary walls of one's own community becomes more likely to flourish in such communities.

Theological educators drawn to the vision of inclusive communities of belonging in which a generative interdependence can thrive will find a rich source of inspiration in the Benedictine spiritual tradition. Community was of central interest to Benedict (480–c. 547) who viewed it as its own school of love for those seeking God. Benedict's insights regarding community are seen best through study of his *Rule*, written in sixth-century Italy, which has become a classic of Christian history. The *Rule of St. Benedict* has had a fifteen-hundred-year run, and it continues to influence scores of Benedictine and Cistercian communities today, and thousands more persons who seek to live elements of its wisdom outside of a monastery context.

Benedict's *Rule* is sensible, reasonable, flexible, and moderate in the direction of practice—all features of community that theological educators do well to consider. The practical realism with which Benedict thought about how effective communities were constituted is evident in the layout and chapter headings of the *Rule* itself. Here one detects his commitment to an egalitarian style of community, his interest in leaders that seek to lead communities rather than drive them, and his conviction that accountability is what protects and galvanizes community.[31] One also observes his keen sensitivity to the diverse situations and needs of people in chapters of the *Rule* like those devoted to "Distribution of Goods according to Need (ch. 34)," "The Sick Brothers" (ch. 36), "The Elderly and Children" (ch. 37), "Brothers Working at a Distance or Traveling" (ch. 50), "The Reception of Guests," and (ch. 53) "Assignment of Impossible Tasks to a Brother" (ch. 68).[32]

Central to a Benedictine way of community is the practice of *hospitality*, described by scholar Esther de Waal as something more than the welcome of the open door: "It is also the open heart and the open mind."[33] Hospitality signals many things: "the need to be reciprocal, to receive as well as to give, and above all to show reverence and respect to the other."[34] Hospitality makes room for the unknown, the other, the surprising, the stranger, and even what is unwanted, as these so often witness to the mystery of God's "livingness," addressing us in ways that invite our narrowness of welcome to expand. In such situations, hospitality "proclaims the immanence of God"[35] in the existential throes of life.

In Benedictine tradition, two connecting elements buttress hospitality. These are commitments to a way of listening and a disposition of humility. The Prologue to the *Rule* begins with the command, "Listen...and incline the ear of the heart."[36] It is an arresting opening, riveting in its starkness. The listening referenced here is more than a hearing. It is a listening that is expectant of a word of God, which may arrive as discerned in a council meeting, in the exhortation of the abbot/abbess, in the offerings of community members old and young, in the porter, in the call of visitors and the poor, in scripture, in communal song, in the natural order. The listener seeks to obey what is heard that is of God. It is impossible to speak of listening in a Benedictine sense without speaking about obedience to the emerging word of God.

One finds Psalm 95:8 inserted into verse 10 of the Prologue of the *Rule*: "Today, **when** you hear his voice, do not harden your hearts!" *Hodie si vocem audieritis, nolite obdurare corda vestra.*[37] Benedict does not assume an "if" here, but rather a "when" with respect to the hearing of God's voice. His confidence in the regular communication of God's "word" to the human is most noteworthy. Commenting on the placement of this verse in the *Rule*, and the fact that it is sung daily in the invitatory,[38] Aquinata Bockman writes, "Every morning this verse rings out like a fanfare calling for a full awakening. Today!"[39] Expectant listening goes hand in hand with the formation of a humble heart, one open to being transformed by this "word," awed by the initiative of God, and willing to stay honest and accountable in community.

Benedictine hospitality with its accompanying way of listening and its stance of humility has much to suggest to theological educators. How will we incline the ear of the heart to difference, to persons' varying abilities, strengths, and needs, and to positions presented that are less favored and not our own? How will we greet people who come into our lives who may stretch us to the limit? And most of all, will we successfully communicate to our students, and from a voice of experience, that in such opportunities, as Joan Chittister assures, "we become more than we were when we began?"[40]

A Summons in the Vision

Proverbs 29:18 reminds scripture readers that "without a vision, people perish." Without a vision, educators waffle. Persons hunger for worthy visions to which they can aspire that will orient and guide practice.

Pausing before three facets of vision embedded in "formative education" and presented in this chapter, theological educators will recognize here congruence with a Christian approach to the person, the world, and the necessity of community in lived faith. And while the term *formative education* itself is of recent vintage, longstanding historical spiritual schools/traditions within Christianity will continue to inform this vision in concrete ways. This essay focuses on but three such spiritual traditions—Ignatian, Salesian, and Benedictine.

Compelling visions generate energy and instill hope. The spiritual vision of formative education does no less, providing a line of sight that encourages movement from vision to mission, while keeping hope for what is formative about theological education very much in focus.

NOTES

1. The threefold description advanced in this article is meant to indicate central elements of the vision of formative education, but it does not purport to be exhaustive in its claims.

2. See Dirk J. Dunfee, Sue Scherer, Ken Sagendorf, James D. Nash, and Cheryl Schwartz, "Revisiting the Promise and Foundations of a Jesuit Education," *Jesuit Higher Education: A Journal* 6, no. 1, Article 10 (2017): 59–65.

3. See Julia Bninski and Jennifer R. Wozniak Boyle, "Cura Personalis as Institutional Practice," *Jesuit Higher Education: A Journal* 9, no. 1, Article 12 (2020): 122–32.

4. "Centennial Visit of Father General Pedro Arrupe," November 11, 1972, box 5, accession no. 001-xx-0013, Centennial Year Records, University Archives, St. Peter's University, Jersey City, NJ.

5. Peter-Hans Kolvenbach, "Cura Personalis," *Review of Ignatian Spirituality* 114 (2007): 10.

6. Kolvenbach, "Cura Personalis," 12.

7. See Barton T. Geger, "Cura Personalis: Some Ignatian Inspirations," *Jesuit Higher Education: A Journal* 3, no. 2, Article 2 (2014): 6–20.

8. Geger, "Cura Personalis: Some Ignatian Inspirations," 17.

9. "Banking education" is an approach to teaching that presumes that the leader in the learning process is the one with all the

information and that students are the passive recipients of this information. Paulo Freire utilized this term bringing strong critique to this way of educating. See Freire, *Pedagogy of the Oppressed*, 50th anniv. ed. (New York: Bloomsbury Academic, 2018).

10. Bninski and Boyle, "Cura Personalis as Institutional Practice," 124.

11. See Nel Noddings, *Caring: A Feminine Approach to Ethics and Moral Education* (Berkeley: University of California Press, 2003).

12. Carol R. Rodgers and Miriam B. Raider-Roth, "Presence in Teaching," *Teachers and Teaching: Theory and Practice* 12, no. 3 (June 2006), 265.

13. Rodgers and Raider-Roth, "Presence in Teaching," 265.

14. See Rodgers and Raider-Roth, "Presence in Teaching," 267–68.

15. Miroslav Volf and Matthew Croasmun, *For the Life of the World: Theology that Makes a Difference* (Grand Rapids, MI: Baker Publishing, 2019), 11.

16. See M. Shawn Copeland, "Weaving Memory, Structuring Ritual, Evoking Mythos: Commemoration of the Ancestors," in *Invitation to Practical Theology: Catholic Visions and Voices*, ed. Claire E. Wolfteich (Mahwah, NJ: Paulist Press, 2014), 125–48.

17. Francis de Sales, *Treatise on the Love of God*, trans. Henry Benedict Mackey (Westminster, MD: Newman Press, 1942), 231.

18. De Sales, *Treatise on the Love of God*, 440–41.

19. Wendy M. Wright, "Salesian Spirituality and the Art of Spiritual Direction," *Studies in Spirituality* 6 (1996), 199.

20. De Sales, *Treatise on the Love of God*, 232.

21. Wright, "Salesian Spirituality," 199.

22. Francis de Sales, *Introduction to the Devout Life* (New York: Vintage Books, 2002), 20.

23. I am grateful to Salesian scholar Wendy Wright for her reminder that gentleness presumes nonviolence, and that gentleness, patience, and humility, sometimes thought of "little virtues," are in fact powerful relational virtues. See Wendy M. Wright, "Prayer in the Salesian Tradition," in *Prayer in the Catholic Tradition: A Handbook of Practical Approaches*, ed. Robert J. Wicks (Cincinnati, OH: Franciscan Media, 2016), 267–80.

24. *Francis de Sales, Jane de Chantal: Letters of Spiritual Direction*, trans. Péronne Marie Thibert, Classics of Western Spirituality (Mahwah, NJ: Paulist Press, 1988), 203.

25. Sharon D. Welch, *After the Protests Are Heard: Enacting Civic Engagement and Social Transformation* (New York: New York University Press, 2019), 16.

26. Welch, *After the Protests Are Heard*, 48.

27. Willie James Jennings, *After Whiteness: An Education in Belonging* (Grand Rapids, MI: Eerdmans, 2020), 10.

28. Jennings, *After Whiteness*, 10.

29. Here Sharon Welch is influenced by a statement made by Cory Booker, U.S. Senator from New Jersey, at the Democratic National Convention in 2016: "We have a Declaration of Independence. But our history sings a much more profound declaration—a Declaration of Interdependence." See Welch, *After the Protests Are Heard*, 16.

30. Welch, *After the Protests Are Heard*, 16.

31. See Columba Stewart, *Prayer and Community: The Benedictine Tradition* (Maryknoll, NY: Orbis Books, 1998).

32. See Benedict, *The Rule of Saint Benedict*, ed. Timothy Fry, Vintage Edition (Collegeville, MN: Order of St. Benedict, 1981).

33. Esther de Waal, *Seeking God: The Way of St. Benedict* (Collegeville, MN: Liturgical Press, 2001), 12.

34. Esther de Waal, *Seeking Life: The Baptismal Invitation of the Rule of St. Benedict* (Collegeville, MN: Liturgical Press, 2009), 31.

35. Laura Swan, *The Benedictine Tradition* (Collegeville, MN: Liturgical Press, 2007), xx.

36. Benedict, *The Rule of St. Benedict*, 3.

37. Benedict, Prologue, *The Rule of St. Benedict*, 3.

38. The invitatory is the psalm or verse that invites persons to prayer.

39. Aquinata Bockmann, *A Listening Community: A Commentary on the Prologue and Chapters 1–3 of Benedict's Rule* (Collegeville, MN: Liturgical Press, 2013), 23.

40. Joan Chittister, *Aspects of the Heart: The Many Paths to a Good Life* (New London, CT: Twenty-Third Publications, 2012), 46.

2

THE WAY OF KNOWING SOUGHT

A Biblical Reflection

Andrew R. Davis

THE BIBLE HAS been in the business of formative theological education for many centuries now. Generations of Jews and Christians have come to know God through the story of Israel coming to know God; their values, perspectives, and ways of action have been shaped by the values, perspectives, and ways of actions of biblical characters. Such formation is no accident of interpretation but a stated purpose within the biblical text itself. At several points in the Old Testament narrative, the Israelites are told to remember a story or law so that they can hand it down to their children and their children's children (Exod 12:26; Deut 4:9–10; 31:13; 32:46; Josh 4:6–7, 21–22).

To these verses we can add the fact that many of the biblical stories as we know them reached their final form during the Babylonian exile (586–539 BCE), when they were collected and edited by exiled Judeans. Whatever the intentions of their original authors may have been, for the exilic community the stories were *torah*, instruction, which (re)taught them who they were, where they came from, and who is the God they worship. Such formation through narrative may never have been more urgent or consoling than it was for the Judeans who had been traumatized by the destruction of Jerusalem and were now separated from their homeland.

In the following essay I will highlight five aspects of theological knowing in the Hebrew Bible. Knowledge of God (1) is to be known by God, (2) is relational, (3) involves covenantal obligations, (4) is embodied, and (5) is contextual. Each element represents a distinctive dimension of the Hebrew verb "to know" (*yada*ʿ), and each is instructive for formative theological education. After illustrating these five aspects of biblical knowing, I will discuss how they have shaped my own approach to teaching the Hebrew Bible at the Boston College School of Theology and Ministry.

We Are Known by God

The phrase "knowledge of God" can be read in two ways; it can mean both our knowledge about God and God's own knowledge (of us). Theological formation in the Bible begins with the latter—with the recognition that we are known by God. This divine knowing is most apparent in the election of Abraham and later Israel for a special relationship with Yhwh.[1] In Genesis 18:19, Yhwh describes Abraham as the one whom "I have known (*yada*ʿ) so that he may instruct his children, his household, and his descendants to keep the way of Yhwh by doing justice and righteousness."[2] Modern translations of this verse often render *yada*ʿ as "chosen" or "singled out," and I don't disagree with these translations because they express a connotation in the Hebrew than is not always captured by the English word *to know*. Divine knowledge is a matter of God reaching out and making a connection to a particular person or a people.

This connection to Abraham continues into the Book of Exodus, where his descendants in Egypt are likewise known by God. Exodus is a dramatic story of liberation and covenant, but it begins with Yhwh knowing Israel. In Exodus 2:25, after an account of Israel's oppression and groaning, we read that "God saw the Israelites and God knew (*yada*ʿ) them," and Yhwh tells Moses, "I have seen the plight of my people in Egypt. I have heard their cry because of their taskmasters; I know (*yada*ʿ) their suffering" (3:7). As in Genesis 18:19, these instances of *yada*ʿ are not always rendered as "to know" (e.g., "took notice of" and "mindful of" in the NRSV and JPS translations). These translations are understandable, but unfortunately, they obscure the correspondence between God's initial knowing and Israel's coming to know Yhwh later in the Exodus story. The biblical authors use the same verb *yada'* for both Yhwh and Israel, and in doing so, they depict Israel's knowledge of God as a response to God's knowing them first.

Another good example of this divine initiative in knowing is Yhwh's call of the prophet Jeremiah, where Yhwh tells him that "before I formed you in the womb, I knew (*yada'*) you / before you were born, I consecrated you / I appointed you a prophet to the nations" (Jer 1:5). Yhwh's knowing of Jeremiah is the foundation of his career as a prophet. Whatever knowledge of God Jeremiah will gain and share with God's people is predicated on the fact that God knew and also formed him first. Translated into theological education today, this feature of biblical knowing invites us to recognize that our theological formation likewise begins with God knowing and forming us. These examples from the Bible remind us that, prior to any program of theological study and formation, students already have a vital source of theology from their previous experience of God.

Knowledge of God Is Relational

In Exodus 2:25 and 3:7, quoted above, Yhwh claims to know Israel and to know its suffering. In these verses Yhwh is not simply making a mental note but is expressing sympathy and solidarity with Israel and a willingness to do something about their dire situation. Indeed, the very next verse contains Yhwh's promise to liberate Israel from its slavery in Egypt (3:8). Equally significant is Yhwh's identification in 3:6 as the God of Abraham, Isaac, and Jacob because this relationship with these ancestors provides the basis for the solidarity Yhwh expresses in the next verse. Taken together, these three verses (3:6–8) highlight another key insight: knowledge of God is inextricable from relationship with God.[3]

In the Exodus story, this dimension of biblical knowing is highlighted by the contrasting portrayals of Yhwh and Pharaoh. At the beginning of the story, the latter is introduced as "a new king who did not know (*yada'*) Joseph" (1:8). This statement indicates not just ignorance of history but also a dissolution of the mutuality that once existed between the Pharaoh and Israel. The bond established by Joseph's service to Egypt has disappeared, and with it went all the benefits Pharaoh had bestowed on Israel (see Gen 41:41–45; 47:7–12). This characterization of Pharaoh as "unknowing" and disconnected continues in Exodus 5, when Moses first asks him to release the Israelites. He replies, "Who is Yhwh? I do not know (*yada'*) Yhwh, and I will not let Israel go" (5:2; cf. Gen 41:37–40).[4]

Whereas Pharaoh is defined in Exodus by his estrangement from Israel and Yhwh, Israel and Yhwh represent the epitome of knowing mutuality. I have already noted Yhwh's foundational knowing of Israel; the story that unfolds from there is one of Israel coming to know Yhwh. When I teach this story, I often ask the class: Why didn't Yhwh simply teleport the Israelites out of Egypt and into the Promised Land? Why go through the rigmarole of the plagues? Why remain in slavery even one more minute, if the ultimate goal is liberation? The narrative's own answer to these questions is Yhwh's desire for Israel to grow in knowledge of their God. This desire is expressed repeatedly throughout Exodus 1—14:

- By this you will know (*yada'*) that I am Yhwh" (7:17).
- ...so that you will know (*yada'*) that I Yhwh am in the midst of the land (8:22).
- ...so that you will know (*yada'*) there is none like me in all the land (9:14).
- ...so that you will know (*yada'*) that I am Yhwh (10:2).

This knowledge culminates in the covenant that Yhwh will establish with Israel at Sinai in Exodus 19—24, which formalizes their relationship. To know God is to be in relationship with God and vice versa; they are two sides of the same coin in the Bible and not just for the generation who fled Egypt and first entered the covenant, but for every generation afterward. Indeed, the purpose of Yhwh's saving actions in Egypt is "so that you may recount in the hearing of your children and children's children the signs that I set forth in Egypt—in order that you will know (*yada'*) that I am Yhwh" (10:2). The Exodus is the story of Israel's formation as the people of God,[5] and all along it was meant to serve as a source of ongoing formation for God's people, including Jews and Christians today. What that story reveals about God's justice and righteousness is a key source of our knowledge about God but also a way to enter into relationship with God.

This relational meaning of *yada'* is hardly unique to the Exodus story. Another instructive source for this meaning is the Book of Hosea. In Hosea 4:1, for example, Yhwh complains that "there is no truth, there is no loyalty (*ḥesed*), there is no knowledge of God (*da'at 'elohim*) in the land," and later in 6:6 Yhwh explains, "I desire loyalty (*ḥesed*), not sacrifice, knowledge of God (*da'at 'elohim*) rather than burnt offerings." Significantly, both verses parallel "knowledge of God" with the Hebrew word *ḥesed*. The latter can be translated in various ways (loving-kindness, steadfast love, goodness, and others), but I prefer "loyalty" because the word signifies fidelity to another within an established relationship, especially a covenantal one; it entails the reciprocal responsibilities between the partners in that relationship (e.g., Yhwh and Israel in Exod 15:13; 20:6; 34:6–7; David and Jonathan in 1 Sam 15:6; 20:8, 14–15; Yhwh and David in 2 Sam 7:15; Ruth and Naomi in Ruth 1:8).[6] The combination of *ḥesed* with *da'at 'elohim* highlights the relational dimension of knowledge of God. Abraham Joshua Heschel captured this meaning well when he wrote in his analysis of Hosea that "the words *daath elohim* mean *sympathy for God*, attachment of the whole person…an act of involvement, attachment or commitment to God."[7]

Knowledge of God Involves Covenantal Obligations

Further insight into this covenantal dimension of divine knowing comes from considering the ancient Near Eastern background of the Hebrew verb *yada'*. Biblical covenants in general are modeled on ancient treaties, and in these treaties the verb *to know* is a technical term of recognition between the treaty partners.[8] This treaty background highlights that covenantal knowledge of God involved obligations on both sides. Knowing God brings Israel life and prosperity but also the expectation that they will reciprocate God's *ḥesed* by serving Yhwh alone and by sharing God's mercy and justice with others. Translated theologically, this aspect of biblical knowing means that as our knowledge of God grows, it obliges us to respond in ways that are faithful to that knowledge.

Take the Decalogue, for example. It begins with Yhwh's self-identification and reminder of Israel's experience of divine rescue

(Exod 20:2), then names the ways Israel is expected to respond to what they have learned about Yhwh's justice. This response involves exclusive devotion to Yhwh (Exod 20:3–11) and care for other members of the human family (Exod 20:12–17), fellow Israelites (mother, father, neighbor) and non-Israelites (resident aliens, slaves) alike. The point is even more explicit in the Deuteronomic version of the Decalogue, where the Sabbath rest for slaves is connected to Yhwh's liberation of Israel when the Israelites were slaves in Egypt (Deut 5:15). The Israelites' experience of Exodus taught them that Yhwh is a God who hears the cry of the oppressed and is committed to liberation from oppression. This is not simply information to be filed away in annals of history: it is living knowledge that Israel must put into practice in its present communities. Further expressions of this insistence on application comes from verses like Exodus 23:9, where Yhwh enjoins Israel: "You shall not oppress a resident alien, for you know the life of an alien from when you were aliens in the land of Egypt" (see also Exod 22:21).

In our own lives we know that relationships are hard work and involve mutual obligations. Our commitments to a spouse, parents, children, friends, colleagues, students, and the like, make demands on our behavior, and according to this aspect of biblical knowing, our relationship with God is no different. Knowledge of God is not self-contained but is embedded within the network of relationships that make up creation; what Israel has learned about God brings new responsibility within that network. Exegetes sometimes classify biblical covenants as conditional or unconditional, but a closer reading shows that all covenants involve expectations and have consequences when those expectations are not met (cf. Amos 3:2).[9]

This aspect of biblical knowing demonstrates the importance of praxis in formative theological education. For students of theology, knowledge of God is an opportunity to deepen their spirituality and enrich their life of faith, but it should not be an end in itself; rather, it shapes our devotion to God and our treatment of others within our religious community and beyond. This outward orientation is captured well in Genesis 18:19, where the verb *yada'* indicates Yhwh's special covenantal relationship with Abraham and the obligations it brings for him and his household: "For him have I known (*yada'*), that he may charge his children and his household after him to keep the way of Yhwh by doing righteousness and justice."[10] This verse encapsulates much of what the Bible offers theological education today. There is the correlation between Abraham's being known by God and his relationship with God, but there is also the insistence that this knowledge be expressed in acts of justice and righteousness by Abraham—and his descendants. Israel's knowing extends outward and is formative for future generations. Its theological education and our own is an ongoing process that is rooted in relationship with God, with each other, and with all of creation.

Knowledge of God Is Embodied

"To know in the biblical sense" is a common English euphemism for sexual intercourse, and it is true that the Hebrew verb "to know" (*yada'*) sometimes refers to sex, as when we learn in Genesis 4:1 that Adam knew Eve and she conceived and bore a son (also Gen 4:17, 25; 19:8; and others). What is less often appreciated is that this sexual meaning of Hebrew *yada'* is rooted in the word's fundamental connotation of relationship.[11] As I have noted earlier, biblical knowledge (*da'at*, from the root *yada'*) is not merely (or even primarily) a matter of intellect and cognition but is the fruit of relationship; it is an embodied knowledge gained through our encounters with others. Sexual knowledge is simply the most intimate instance of such an encounter.

Intercourse, however is not the only way that knowledge is embodied in the Bible. A beautiful illustration is Psalm 139, in which the speaker uses the verb *yada'* six times (and the noun *da'at* once) to celebrate God's intimate knowledge of her. Especially noteworthy is the description in verses 13–16:

> You created my inward parts;
> you knit me together in my mother's womb.
> I praise you, for I am awesomely and wonderfully made.
> Wonderful are your works; that I know [*yōda'at*] very well.
> My bones were not hidden from you when I was formed in secret,
> When I was woven in the depths of the earth.
> Your eyes beheld me as an embryo.

This description speaks to God's detailed knowledge of us from the beginning of our existence, specifically our existence as embodied beings. But just as significant in this passage is the way the speaker's being bodily known by God becomes a source of her own theology. Because God knows her in this way, she is able to declare her knowledge of God: "Wonderful are your works" (which include the speaker herself).

Psalm 139's account of being known in the womb is reminiscent of the biblical prophets who likewise recognize their connection to God as early as the womb (Isa 49:1; Jer 1:5). Indeed, the prophetic books of the Hebrew Bible also illustrate this embodied knowing of God. Biblical prophets come to know God through their body and mediate that knowledge to others in bodily ways. The prophet Balaam, for example, is described as one who "knows knowledge (*yada' da'at*) of the Most High" by hearing the divine word and seeing visions; his knowledge is a sensory experience and leads to a bodily response, namely, falling down (Num 24:16).

Balaam is hardly unique in this regard. In the Books of Jeremiah and Ezekiel, bodily knowing is often expressed through the symbol of the heart, which in the Hebrew Bible is the organ associated with the will. Jeremiah preaches words of judgment and feels in his own heart the pain he knows is coming for the people of Judah (Jer 4:19; 8:18; 23:9), but the heart is also the place where renewed relationship between Yhwh and Israel will begin. God declares in Jeremiah 24:7, "I will give them a heart to know (*yada'*) me, for I am Yhwh. They will be my people, and I will be their God, for they shall return to me with their whole heart." The verb *yada'* and the covenantal formula ("They will be my people, and I will be their God") express again the correlation between knowledge and relationship, but this passage also involves the body as the locus of that knowledge (see also Jer 31:33).

In the Book of Ezekiel we find the heart again used to symbolize the renewal of divine knowledge and relationship (e.g., 11:19; 36:26), but a unique example of embodied knowledge in the book is its description in chapter 37 of dry bones brought back to life. Yhwh says to the bones through the prophet, "I will give you sinews and bring flesh upon your body; I will cover you in skin and put breath in you, so that you will live and know (*yada'*) that I am Yhwh" (Ezek 37:6). The story of the dry bones, like the verses from Jeremiah, insists that knowledge of God is not a disembodied abstraction; we do not need to escape our bodies in order to know and be in relationship with God.[12] Rather, our bodies are the locus of divine encounter and knowledge, the place where our knowledge of God begins and where God renews us for further relationship. Translated into the work of formative theological education, this aspect of biblical knowing invites us to teach theology not simply as an intellectual project but one that involves our entire embodied being.[13]

Knowledge of God Is Contextual

Contextuality is another feature of biblical knowing that is instructive for formative theological education. We have already seen that the Exodus story exemplifies both the relational and covenantal aspects of biblical knowing, but just as important is the way that Israel *grows* in knowledge of and relationship with God. This deepening intimacy is most apparent in the revelation of the divine name Yhwh in Exodus 6:

> God spoke to Moses and said to him: "I am Yhwh. I appeared to Abraham, to Isaac, and to Jacob as El Shaddai, but by my name Yhwh I did not make myself known (*yada'*) to them. I established my covenant with them...and I have remembered my covenant....I will take you as my people, and I will be your God. You shall know (*yada'*) that I am Yhwh your God, who has brought you out from under the burdens of the Egyptians" (6:2–3, 5, 7).

Besides reinforcing the relationality of *yada'* and its covenantal connotations, this passage shows Yhwh's desire to draw Moses and Israel into deeper relationship. By revealing the divine name, Yhwh is sharing an intimate detail that was unknown to Abraham, Isaac, and Jacob. (There is a source critical issue here, since other Pentateuchal strands have been using the name Yhwh all along. For the Priestly writer, however, the revelation is a momentous occasion.)

The revelation shows that knowledge of God is a dynamic process that unfolds over time and in which we participate according to our own context. Just as the unique circumstances of the Israelites in Egypt required a new kind of divine availability and yielded new insights about God, so also the unique circumstances of our lives hold the potential for new theological insights. Such knowledge is not divorced from previous knowledge; after all, Yhwh is still the God of Abraham,

Isaac, and Jacob, and Yhwh's revelation and promises to those ancestors are still valid. But knowledge of God in the Exodus story is also not a replication of that earlier revelation. Likewise, we have the benefit of the knowledge of the generations before us as well as the opportunity to add to that knowledge by reflecting on our relationship with God in our time and place.[14]

This dynamic process of knowing God is also illustrated in Israel's covenant tradition. Although we often think of biblical covenants proceeding in a linear progression, the Old Testament features a plurality of "everlasting covenants" (*berit 'olam*), each suited to its particular moment in salvation history. The first is God's covenant with Noah, his descendants, and all living creatures of the ark—indeed with the entire earth (Gen 9:8–17). A few chapters later Yhwh chooses Abraham and Sarah for a special relationship (Gen 15, 17). Though narrower in scope, the Abrahamic covenant maintains the universal horizon established by the Noahide covenant (cf. 12:3). The Sinaitic covenant (Exod 19–24), which Yhwh makes with Abraham's descendants, maintains the particularity of their ancestor's covenant but introduces an important change. Yhwh still guarantees prosperity for his covenant partner, expressed here as steadfast love (*ḥesed*), but now names the particular ways that he expects Israel to reciprocate that loyalty. Finally, the advent of kingship offers Yhwh a new way to be in relationship with Israel, and so Yhwh establishes a covenant with David, which, like the Sinaitic covenant, is based on divine *ḥesed* (2 Sam 7:15). This brief survey of biblical covenants shows that, far from being one-size-fits-all, covenants are contextual. As the biblical narrative unfolds and God's people encounter new circumstances, God is willing and able to find new ways to be in relationship with them. What worked after the flood cannot be cut-and-pasted onto the tablets of Moses, and the beginning of kingship likewise calls for new kind of covenant. Diversity among biblical covenants is a good thing because it shows that, while God remains constant in fidelity, justice, and mercy, God is also responsive to the changing needs of God's people.[15]

According to this biblical model, knowledge of God entails reflecting on God's presence in our lives and thinking about that presence in the context of our religious tradition. We don't grow in knowledge of God by withdrawing from our daily lives or transcending the world around us but by making our daily lives the very data of our theological reflection. In my view, this approach is consistent with the goals of formative theological education, which invites students to bring the totality of their lives to bear on their theological questions. The source of Israel's knowledge of God was their (and their ancestors') experience of God and relationship with God. They committed this experiential knowledge to written texts so that future generations could also be shaped by their experience of Yhwh. Their experience provides a framework for interpreting Yhwh's ongoing presence in Israel and the wider creation. In this way, the biblical tradition of knowing God opens our eyes and hearts to the ways that God has acted in the lives of earlier generations and primes us for the knowledge that may be revealed in our own contexts.

Biblical Knowing in the Classroom Today

Having outlined five key features of theological knowledge in the Hebrew Bible, I conclude this essay by reflecting on what biblical knowing offers theological education today. In my view, the five features align well with the aims of formative education, and I share here some examples of how the biblical perspective has influenced my own pedagogical practices.

The first two features—knowledge as being known by God and in relationship with God—speak to the recognition that the knowledge exchanged in the classroom is (or should be) one part of a larger knowing that encompasses all facets of a student's life. I assume that outside of my classroom students are encountering and deepening their relationship with God—through other classes, personal prayer, liturgies, spiritual direction, volunteer ministries, and so on. In all these ways, students are coming to recognize God's presence in their lives and work, and a theological education that is formative will foster the integration of these various ways of knowing God. The main goal of my biblical courses is not content delivery but connecting course content to what students already know about God and what they are learning outside of my classroom.

In my experience, the best way to make these connections is to invite students to make them and then give them the time and space to do so. For example, I start every class with a prayer, and in my first year of teaching, I offered all of the prayers. After a year of struggling to find new material for each class meeting, I was inspired to hand the task over to the students who would take turns leading prayers. The results have been astounding, and I sometimes think that the couple minutes of prayer at the beginning of class are the most important thing that happens in the classroom that day. The prayer is an opportunity for students to share their spirituality with the class, and it tells the students that their ways of knowing and being known by God have a place in the classroom. It is a reminder that the theological knowledge imparted in a given class is set against a larger backdrop of relationship with God, and I have been amazed over the years at the ways that students link their opening prayer to course content. Some even begin their prayer by saying they chose it in light of recent class discussions. Those are moments I could never create myself, but by giving students the invitation and space and by trusting in the knowledge they are developing in other parts of their lives, I let them become agents of their own formative education.

The last three aspects of biblical knowing—knowledge as covenantal, embodied, and contextual—call to mind the importance of getting students to think about potential applications of the knowledge they are gaining in the classroom. Several of my courses include an exegesis presentation as one of the required assignments; students take turns researching a biblical passage and presenting the fruits of their research to their classmates. After detailing the various historical and literary aspects of the passage, students are asked to share a pastoral setting where their exegesis would resonate. Like the opening prayer in class, this practice recognizes the need to connect knowledge inside and outside the classroom, but whereas the prayer brings the outside knowledge in, the exegesis presentation aims to take classroom knowledge out into the world.

When students are preparing their presentations, I tell them that the more specific they make their pastoral application, the better. They should choose an audience or setting that is meaningful to them and which they know well. It is unlikely that they will uncover a new insight into the historical or literary understanding of their passage, but because of their unique backgrounds and vocations, students can reveal a new pastoral dimension of the text. This part of the presentation recognizes that students' knowledge of God is not only for their personal formation but is meant to be embodied in their ministerial practice. There is no formula for this pastoral application because each student comes from a different context, and each application is specific to that context. Collectively, these pastoral applications highlight contextuality as a value in theological education. By hearing their classmates consider the meaning of a biblical text within their communities and ministerial settings, students come to see their own community and ministerial setting as indispensable to the meaning of their exegesis passage.

These are just some of the ways that biblical ways of knowing God have influenced my pedagogy. They are not the only ways or even the best ways, but they do show how biblical knowing is aligned with the goals and methods of formative theological education. The model offered by the Old Testament is one in which knowledge of God is not so much the product of intellectual study as it is an experience of God who meets us in our everyday lives, and this knowledge makes claims on our relationship with God and other people. As theological educators, we are called to help students weave together these various threads into a single fabric. To do so is to align ourselves with the theological perspective of the biblical writers and their ancient audiences.

NOTES

1. In this essay I retain the divine name Yhwh rather than change it to "the Lord." Besides better reflecting the biblical text, the practice reinforces a point made in this chapter. Yhwh is the proper name of the God of Israel, and its use shows God's commitment to intimate relationship with Israel. Yhwh wants to be "on a first name basis" with them (cf. Exod 6:2–8). In deference to the Jewish tradition of not speaking this holy name aloud, I have omitted its vowels.

2. All translations are my own.

3. G. Johannes Botterweck and J. Bergman, "יָדַע *yāḏa'*," in *Theological Dictionary of the Old Testament*, ed. G. Johannes Botterweck and Helmer Ringgren, trans. David E. Green (Grand Rapids, MI: Eerdmans, 1986), 5:469–70.

4. See Dru Johnson, *Biblical Knowing: A Scriptural Epistemology of Error* (Cambridge: James Clarke, 2013), 68–70.

5. Cf. Isa 43:21, which describes the Exodus as a process by which Yhwh "formed (*yṣr*) a people for myself." This verb is most often used in the Hebrew Bible to denote the shaping of clay into pottery.

6. See Katharine Doob Sakenfeld, *The Meaning of* ḥesed *in the Hebrew Bible: A New Inquiry*, HSM 17 (Missoula, MT: Scholar's Press, 1978).

7. Abraham J. Heschel, *The Prophets* (Peabody, MA: Hendrickson, 2010), 1:59. First published by Harper and Row, 1962.

8. See Herbert B. Huffmon, "The Treaty Background of Hebrew *yāda'*," *BASOR* 181 (1966): 31–37; and Herbert B. Huffmon and Simon Parker, "A Further Note on the Treaty Background of Hebrew *yāda'*," *BASOR* 184 (1966): 36–38.

9. Sometimes the covenants of Noah (Gen 9), Abraham (Gen 15, 17), and David (2 Sam 7) are considered unconditional. But in Gen 9:4–6, humanity is expected to curb its violent ways; in Gen 17:1, Abraham is told to "walk in before [God] and be blameless"; and in 2 Sam 7:14, Yhwh expects fidelity and will redress any wrongdoing by David's descendants. See further Andrew R. Davis, "A Biblical View of Covenants Old and New," *Theological Studies* 81, no. 3 (2020): 631–48.

10. On the significance of this verse in terms of covenant and election, see Joel S. Kaminsky, *Yet I Loved Jacob: Reclaiming the Biblical Concept of Election* (Nashville: Abingdon Press, 2007), 137.

11. Dru Johnson goes even further to describe this embodied knowledge as a kind of sacramentality. See *Biblical Knowing*, 36–39.

12. For the theme of knowledge in Ezekiel, see Walther Zimmerli, "Knowledge of God according to the Book of Ezekiel," in *I Am Yahweh*, ed. Walter Brueggemann, trans. Douglas W. Stott (Atlanta: John Knox, 1982), 29–98. Originally published in German in 1954. In this essay, Zimmerli emphasizes that knowledge of God in Ezekiel is not something that happens in the human interior but is a response to God's (saving) actions.

13. Cf. David Arthur Lambert, who argues that biblical knowing involves "a material form of encounter" rather than a psychological process ("Refreshing Philology: James Barr, Supersessionism, and the State of Biblical Words," *Biblical Interpretation* 24, no. 3 [July 2016]: 340–41).

14. In this Roman Catholic tradition, the Dogmatic Constitution on Divine Revelation, *Dei Verbum*, expressed well this biblical tradition of ongoing revelation: "For there is a growth in the understanding of the realities and the words which have been handed down. This happens through the contemplation and study made by believers, who treasure these things in their hearts (see Luke, 2:19, 51) through a penetrating

understanding of the spiritual realities which they experience, and through the preaching of those who have received through Episcopal succession the sure gift of truth" (Vatican Council II, Dogmatic Constitution on Divine Revelation, *Dei Verbum* [November 18, 1965], §8, https://www.vatican.va/archive/hist_councils/ii_vatican_council/documents/vat-ii_const_19651118_dei-verbum_en.html).

15. For more on this topic, see Andrew R. Davis, "A Biblical View of Covenants Old and New," in *Theological Studies* 81, no. 3 (September 2020): 634–35.

3

FORMATIVE FACTORS IN TALKING ABOUT GOD

Richard Lennan

"TALKING ABOUT GOD" functions often as a definition of *theology*. The characterization is straightforward and faithful to the two Greek terms—*theos* and *logos*—that combine to name the discipline. These virtues notwithstanding, the definition provides little specificity, shedding no light on the details of such talk. Beyond interest in who might do this talking, what makes it possible, and how it proceeds, a curious inquirer might wonder whether and how discourse about God affects those who engage in it: Can talking about God stimulate, for example, openness to new modes of interpreting life and participating in the world? This question is surely a crucial one for theological educators.

To clarify the particularity of theology, including its potential as an agent of formation for both teachers and learners, this chapter delves into three, interrelated features that are integral to the discipline. The three aspects are the decentering impact of a focus on God, the need for receptivity to what God initiates, and the implications of membership in a community that has God at its center. In addressing these themes, the chapter will detail some dynamics of doing theology, while also highlighting how theology, and so theological education, might shape those who talk about God.

The Decentering God

Human beings talk about myriad topics. Indeed, whether the theme is food, other people, or anything else from the boundless array of possibilities, talking engages much of life in the everyday world. Typical of human discourse is a subject talking about an object, a person talking about a thing. In this framework, it is possible, perhaps even usual, that the speaker remains unaffected by either the subject matter or the activity of talking about it. If this were true of talking about God, theology would be akin to discussing cryptocurrencies or subatomic particles, both of which are issues unlikely to make demands on the speakers or lead them to reconsider their own priorities and practices. With the goal of demonstrating that the work of theology is neither indicative of a fascination with an obscure topic nor something that enables participants to remain totally dispassionate, this section considers the subject matter of theological discourse: God.

Theology is no less a human activity than other forms of talking, but the God who is its focus is unique. God is not an object of measurable dimensions, and certainly not a reality amenable to human control. Most significantly of all, the God around whom all theological discourse revolves is far from being a peer of those doing the talking. The prophet Isaiah presents the difference between God and human beings in stark fashion: "For my thoughts are not your thoughts, / nor are your ways my ways, says the Lord. / For as the heavens are higher than the earth, / so are my ways higher than your ways / and my thoughts than your thoughts" (Isa 55:8–9). This fundamental difference between God and humanity is the foundation of theology as a formative activity. As such, its importance ripples out into theological education.

In an echo of the biblical depiction, Karl Rahner contends that even the word *God* differs from all other words. Unlike *broom* or *desk*, words that capture their object comprehensively, *God* is not a word that delineates or defines. Rahner claims that the word *God*

> is itself the final word before wordless and worshipful silence in the face of the ineffable mystery. It is the word which must be spoken at the conclusion of all speaking....It is an almost ridiculously exhausting and demanding word. If we

> were not hearing it in *this way*...we would have heard something which has nothing in common with the true word "God" but its phonetic sound....The concept "God" is not a grasp of God by which a person masters the mystery, but it is letting oneself be grasped by the mystery that is present and yet ever distant.[1]

Since *God* does not confine its referent within hard-edged borders that any interested party might come to know exhaustively, talking about God will differ from the confident discourse that such borders facilitate. Notably, "each of the great religious traditions," intent on doing justice to God, "has had its own procedures for protecting us from the illusion that the Holy One can be thus pinned down, classified, given a proper name."[2] What is common to these traditions is their recognition of God's transcendence, of the mystery of God as the one who is and will remain beyond humanity's grasp. This radical difference between God and humanity has consequences for the whole process of thinking and talking about God: "God simply cannot be thought of without this idea irritating and disrupting the immediate interests of the one who is trying to think it."[3] God's transcendence, in short, will always thwart humanity's efforts to say the final word about God.

The first formative element in the practice of theological education, therefore, is the decentering of the person talking. Unlike cartographers who map a previously unexplored territory, be it a tract of land or the human genome, teachers of theology have not "mastered" their subject, have not exhausted all that "God" conveys. At its best, then, the study of theology engages teachers and learners with the "more," the mystery, of God.

Since "God as God, ground, support, and goal of all, is illimitable mystery who, while immanently present, cannot be measured, manipulated, or controlled," no theology has the final word about God.[4] As a formative factor, God's transcendence presents humanity—theologians included—with a choice between dwelling resolutely on "the little island of our so-called knowledge" or plunging into "the ocean of the infinite mystery."[5] Every encounter with God exposes its recipients to "a power interrupting our constant temptations to delude ourselves at a level more fundamental than any conscious error; a power gradually but really transforming old habits."[6] The interruptive quality of every human experience of God means that all thinking and talking about God "invites consideration, discussion, revision, change" in those who engage in this thinking and talking.[7] The fact that God "enters as a moment of discontinuity into a larger, already established context" likewise implies that theological reflection can be a stimulus for questioning and reviewing customary ways of acting.[8]

The potential of theology for questioning and expanding worldviews is a further corollary of the discipline's focus on God. Alert to God's transcendence, theology probes "those aspects of religious practice which pull in the direction of ideological distortion, those things which presuppose that there is a mode of religious utterance wholly beyond the risks of conversation, a power beyond resistance, a perspective that leaves nothing out…it will also challenge the notion that these are the terms in which *God* is to be imagined."[9] As a formative endeavor in the context of communities of faith, theology helps to ensure that the church's worship, beliefs, and ways of living lead more deeply into the mystery of God, rather than promoting something less than God.

Clearly, theologians themselves, if they are not to fall victim to their own "ideological distortions," must respect the limits of their own insights. Any approach to theology that might claim to say the final word about God, and any form of theological education that diminishes God's transcendence, veers toward idolatry. Idolatry substitutes for the creator God a "god" whom humanity itself creates and directs. Not surprisingly perhaps, this temptation is one with a long history. Israel's worship of "an image of a calf" (Exod 32:1–6) serves as the usual point of reference for idolatry. That incident, however, is only the most egregious instance of a practice to which human beings have often succumbed, as both numerous other biblical instances and the church's history record.

The temptation to idolatry persists because it is demanding to assent to a God not subject to human control, a God who summons believers to conversion. Idols, on the other hand, leave undisturbed the worldview of their creators. Formative theology, in reflecting the God who eludes human control, promotes the God-given capacity of human beings to expand their worldview, while also embracing more generous and compassionate ways of living. In this way, theology not only does justice to God, but can be a beacon indicating possibilities for a more just and humane society. These possibilities may appeal beyond the theological community.

The effective teaching of theology respects the mystery of God, but can be the catalyst for a deepening insight into this mystery. Such awareness arises through a dialogue between the experience of participants and the wisdom of texts and traditions that expound on and interpret the manifold experience of encountering the transcendent God. With their foundation in the transcendent God, these texts and traditions, far from being unyielding obstacles to change or simply guardians of the status quo, can stimulate new questions and the quest for greater personal and communal authenticity in responding to God. The riches characteristic of a tradition of faith can underpin the conversion that generates new forms of behavior, forms better able to embody what God enables.

Engaging traditions of reflection on God is an additional indicator of the decentering constitutive of faith and of theological education. Since the formation and transmission of traditions is the legacy of communities, not merely individuals, traditions of faith are a reminder that no individual can represent the sum of all experiences of God—an emphasis that will also feature in the discussion of community that the final section of this essay will develop.

Theological educators responsive to the limits of their own experience and understanding will also acknowledge the stimulus that "the world" can provide for theologians. Insights about God, and the movement of God in creation and human society, can come, even if "anonymously," from science, literature, and other forms of human knowing. Every witness to transcendence, to the presence in history of all that human genius and technological skill cannot conquer, reinforces the difference between God and humanity. These witnesses buttress the awareness that no claims about God, irrespective of their source, will ever be adequate to the fullness of God.

With all that challenges the self-sufficiency of theological endeavors, talking about God might seem to be a futile exercise, one best avoided since it is it unlikely either to "clarify" God or contribute meaningfully to human existence. What saves theology from pointlessness, what establishes its possibility and gives substance to its claims, is the fact that God, without loss of transcendence, takes the initiative in addressing humanity. Thus, the talking about God that defines theology is essentially a response to God's self-communication. Just as God's transcendence challenges theologians to accept their decentering, the pivotal role that God's self-disclosure plays in theology's discourse establishes the second formative characteristic of theology: the need for the receptivity to God's self-revelation. This receptivity locates theology as a facet of the practice of faith.

Faithful Receptivity to Grace

Receptivity to God's self-revelation dispels fears that God is inaccessible or unapproachable. Likewise, this receptivity enables theologians to deepen their own understanding of the life-giving nature of God, and of God's generative stance toward creation. This deepening furthers theological education as a formative endeavor.

It is important to note that the God of mystery and the God of revelation are the one God. As this section will demonstrate, God's self-revelation does not detract from God's mystery and certainly does not reduce God to an object in the world. If anything, revelation amplifies God's mystery, underscoring that human experience of God does not reduce God's "otherness." From this base, theological education can promote conversion to ways of living that reflect a faithful response to the life-giving God.

Revelation is God's free act. Human beings can neither compel nor direct the time and mode of this self-disclosure. God, nonetheless, does choose to be accessible to human beings: "from the fullness of his love, [God] addresses men and women as his friends, and lives among them, in order to invite and receive them into his own company."[10] It is this self-communication of God that provides the rationale for theology, whose own talking about God is a response to God's invitation to a relationship.

This relationship, which arises from the meeting of God's self-disclosure and humanity's response, the response that "faith" encapsulates, is formative. A key implication of faithful receptivity to God's self-disclosure is that believers, as Pope Francis stresses, "must be ready to let [themselves] be led, to come out of [themselves] and to find the God of perpetual surprises."[11] As the stimulus for faith, God's revelation opens possibilities that exceed what human capacities can accomplish. Faith invites its practitioners to take up new ways of interacting with each other and the world beyond themselves, ways that God's ongoing self-giving in grace empowers. In addition, faith in God draws believers beyond the present, challenging any tendencies to absolutize a particular moment of history as being the apogee of what human beings might achieve through the God at work in them.

The link between the movement of God's grace and faith clarifies how faith can be formative, including for the work of theology. "Grace" encapsulates the manifold forms of God's presence in history, including God's invitation to a relationship with God. As God's self-bestowal, grace gives life to humanity and to all of God's creatures. Grace is not a "thing" and certainly not quantifiable: grace is the self-expression of the God who is other than "a static, distant, non-interactive God."[12] Theology itself is unimaginable outside of grace, outside of the conviction that relationship with God sustains all aspects of life in the world. For this reason, formative theological education must be attuned to God's engagement with the world.

The omnipresence of grace enables talking about God to be more than simply reflection on private experiences or individual lives. An authentic theology must always include talking about the world that depends on God. This stipulation can save theology from escaping into abstractions, and also distinguish fruitful theological education from the activity of designing ivory towers. Just as the properly formative character of theology respects the decentering God of encounters with God, so too it opens its practitioners to the graced world. An appreciation of grace in the world helps to form people of faith, and so theologians, for dialogue between and among religions and worldviews. Dialogue, as Pope Francis attests in *Fratelli tutti*, can serve the "grand ideals that make life more beautiful and worthwhile."[13] Formative theology promotes such dialogue.

Analyses of grace can highlight the ways in which God's self-communication attunes itself to the needs and capacities of human beings. Since "God moves through human ways of knowing, according to the mode of the soul, according to the way the human person is made," human experience is never alien to God.[14] The fact that God "does not violate our deepest needs but fulfills slowly in our life situations our most profound desires for reassurance, unconditional love, tenderness, and special regard," identifies a God who attracts rather than coerces.[15] Grace promotes the need for, and opportunities to practice, a "disinterested concern for others, and the rejection of every form of self-centeredness and self-absorption."[16] This relational nature of grace, a quality inseparable from the fact that grace is God's self-bestowal, draws recipients into a deeper communion with God, other people, and the whole of God's creation, all of which are the raw materials of theology.

This inextricable link between grace and life in the world indicates that the measure of any theology can never be solely the force of its logic. In fact, a theology that furthers the life of faith, and in so doing enriches all the contexts in which believers live, will be one that is primarily God-centered while also promoting ways of living appropriate to the faithful reception of grace. For this reason, people of faith, even as they are "to seek and value the things that are above," are to show "not less, but greater commitment to working with everyone for the establishment of a more human world."[17]

Ways of living indicative of this dual commitment can include acceptance of the need for conversion from all that fails to reflect grace and so distorts God's presence in the world. It is important to note that a grace-centered theology is not irrational, and certainly not disdainful of human reason, but views reason in relation to grace: "Illumined by faith, reason is set free from the fragility and limitations deriving from the disobedience of sin and finds the strength required to rise to the knowledge of the Triune God."[18] Consistent with this emphasis, formative theological education is more than an exercise of the intellect. In promoting openness to God and God's grace in the world, theological education can nurture a commitment to "'building' history," a commitment inherent in faith in the self-communicating God.[19]

Just as revelation showcases God's commitment to the thriving of the whole of creation, theologians must ensure that their descriptions of God are equally life-affirming. Consequently, teachers of theology, at every level, must eschew any imagery or description that depicts God as "'the truly real' which like a vampire draws to himself and so to speak sucks out the proper reality of things different from himself."[20] A more accurate summary of God's self-communication in grace is that "the nearer one comes to God, the more real one becomes; the more God grows in and before one, the more independent one becomes oneself."[21] A theology that proceeds from receptivity to God's self-revelation is likely to do justice to the God who promotes humanity's well-being, both in the present and future.

This life-giving God is central to the biblical portrayal of God's self-communication that focuses on the covenants that God initiates with Israel, covenants that can secure Israel's well-being in the present and future. At the heart of the covenants is God's all-embracing promise: "I will walk among you, and will be your God, and you shall be my people" (Lev 26:12).[22] Since God provides the impetus for the covenants, God also assumes responsibility for maintaining them in good order. Even as God admonishes Israel's failures to be faithful to the covenants, God continues to encourage hope for the future: "I am God, and there is no one like me, declaring the end from the beginning and from ancient times things not yet done" (Isa 46:9–10). The God of the covenants, then, is more than a means to security in the present; the God of the covenants is life-giving across the past, present, and future.[23]

In the Christian context, the life-giving reality of God finds its fullest expression in Jesus Christ. Jesus preaches a compassionate, forgiving God. Even more, he enacts this God by healing, feeding, and reconciling those broken by their own failures or by socioreligious standards that marginalized many people: "With a tenderness which never disappoints…[Jesus] makes it possible for us to lift up our heads and to start anew."[24] Jesus does not castigate the broken for their brokenness—"neither do I condemn you" (John 8:11)—but provides people with the opportunity to begin again. What Jesus models for formative theological education is the importance of amplifying the hope that is intrinsic to receptivity to God.

Hope is inseparable from the belief that the God who brings all life into being will ensure an outcome for all living things other than a decline into emptiness and futility: "For surely I know the plans I have for you, says the LORD, plans for your welfare and not for harm, to give you a future with hope" (Jer 29:11). Faith-formed hope "has God as its primary object, and in particular our right relationship with God and eternal life. It looks forward to the full coming of God's kingdom. And it has as its basis God's person and promises."[25] For Christians, hope has its source in the life, death, and resurrection of Jesus, in the immeasurable self-emptying of God. In detailing and illuminating God's self-giving, theological education can help to nurture this hope that expresses faith in God and nourishes humanity's own self-giving.

Hope is not a cheap virtue, not a form of wishful thinking. Hope, as an expression of trust that is integral to relationship with God, is inseparable from the self-emptying and risk-taking that embodies response to the God who exceeds humanity's control. This hope, then, displays qualities characteristic of all genuine human relationships:

> The act of self-commitment to the other has a radical, absolute, unconditional quality by no means adequately founded or based on the antecedent grounds for that act....In this self-abandonment, once all antecedent considerations, verifications and demands of reasonableness and legitimation are posited—one ventures more, and *must* venture more, than these grounds seem to justify.[26]

For Christian theology, hope, as noted above, is not merely a theory, but has an inextricable connection with God's self-revelation and God's ongoing presence in grace. This presence of God, a presence that occurs through Jesus Christ and the Holy Spirit, forms and sustains the church as the community of faith. To elaborate on this conviction, the final section of the chapter will highlight the formative role of the community of faith, and its place in theological education.

Formation within the Pilgrim Community of Faith

In the history of Israel, faithfulness to God often required that the people be willing to move, literally and not merely figuratively—"Go from your country and your kindred and your father's house to the land that I will show you" (Gen 12:1). Jesus too spends much of his life on "the road" (Luke 9:51–62). It is by becoming companions with Jesus on the road that the disciples are challenged to learn, for example, that being "first" in God's eyes is not about self-aggrandizement (Mark 9:30–37; Matt 20:17–28). The disciples also learn what it means to be a herald of "the good news" (Luke 9:1–6) in the world. As Jesus moves from place to place, he makes clear that the call to "follow" him (Mark 1:17) involves movement. Not surprisingly, this call is not always a welcome one. The call to "movement" inseparable from intimacy with Jesus could lead to the rejection of Jesus, as it did for the wealthy man who feared the loss of his riches (Mark 10:17–22). Jesus, however, does not dilute the demands of discipleship to increase the number of his followers.

Since Christian faith is not reducible to acceptance of certain "truths," but is the embrace of discipleship, of walking the road with Jesus, the challenge of the person and message of Jesus is as much alive in the twenty-first century as in the first. Acknowledging the dying and rising that Christian discipleship involves is an irreducible component of authentic theology. This fact makes doing theology in the Christian context as confronting for theologians themselves as their work often is for those who study it. Still, Christianity neither begins with the cost of discipleship nor focuses exclusively on the cross. Authentic Christian theology, like the faith from which it proceeds, has its grounding in God's self-giving, in the pervasive presence of God's grace in the world. It is the graced relationship of faith that can shape the work of the theologian and the reception of theology within the Christian community.

The indispensable role that formative encounters with grace plays in both Christian discipleship as a whole and the work of theology brings into focus the Holy Spirit, the agent of grace and so of formation. The Holy Spirit, who completes the revelation of the trinitarian God, calls people to follow Christ, and leads their pilgrimage to the fullness of God's reign. Most significantly, the Spirit fulfills these roles by forming the disciples of Christ into a community.

The notion of a community of faith is not an arbitrary imposition by the Holy Spirit, but illustrates that God's self-communication attunes itself to the reality of human life. Part of this reality is its embodiment, its expression in time and place, while another aspect of it is that human beings are not monads, not isolated individuals living an entirely private existence that does not intersect other people. From this perspective, human community, a reflection of God's trinitarian life, "provides the overall horizon of understanding within which human experience begins to make sense."[27]

For Christians, it is the church that expresses the communal life of faith. As challenging as life in the ecclesial community can be on many levels, Christianity's creedal profession of faith identifies the church as an irreducible component of God's self-revelation in history. As Pope Francis phrases it, faith "is not simply an individual decision which takes place in the depths of the believer's heart, nor a completely private relationship between the 'I' of the believer and the divine 'Thou,' between an autonomous subject and God. By its very nature, faith is open to the 'We' of the Church; it always takes place within her communion."[28]

The church is not a community with an answer to every question. In fact, the church can be faithful only through a willingness to listen to "what the Spirit is saying to the churches" (Rev 2:7, 11, 17, 29; 3:6, 13, 22). In other words, the church as a whole, and in all that manifests the believing community—theologians included—must remain open to conversion, to a more faithful following of Jesus. This faithfulness is inseparable from discerning the movement of the Spirit who is operative in the present moment, while also calling God's people toward the fullness of God's reign. Theological education can nourish for the Christian community the willingness to trust that "the one who began a good work among you will bring it to completion by the day of Jesus Christ" (Phil 1:6).

The great strength of theology done from within the community of faith is the breadth and depth of resources available for this theology. Those resources include the word of God in Scripture—"which ought to be the very soul of all theology"[29]—the liturgy and sacramental life, and the extensive tradition of faith as has taken flesh in a host of practices. These practices—forms of prayer and devotion, but also the community of saints, and a plethora of teachings on justice in the world—express the community's response to grace in its inner life and its manner of participation in the wider life of the world.

Christian faith must remain attentive to the movement of the Spirit's grace in every time and place, but must not succumb to every transient fashion in the wider society. Faithfully creative reception of the church's living tradition, a reception that formative theological education can aid, enables the Christian community to participate constructively in history, while looking beyond the limits of history.

Life in the community of faith offers many challenges for theologians and theological educators no less than for other Christians. The fact that no member of the church designs and enacts the community of their dreams nor begins the church anew on the basis of their own preferences largely guarantees that the ecclesial community will be a site of frustrations. In addition, aspects of the church's life, including the functioning of its structures, can fail to be responsive to all that the Spirit enables, as the clerical sexual abuse crisis has made painfully clear in recent decades.

The theology that emerges from the myriad settings of the ecclesial community cannot guarantee its own righteousness or proclaim its own comprehensiveness. Paradoxically, these limitations bear witness to the enduring importance of the three formative factors this chapter has explored. No theology will ever outgrow its need to renounce any pretensions to defining God comprehensively. Nor can theology legitimately abandon its dependence on all that God's self-disclosure through Christ and the Spirit illuminates about God. Since it is the community of faith that mediates God's self-disclosure, theology will always have its basis in the community's faith. In being attentive to these three framing principles, theology can be formative. Structures of education that give voice to this formative theology will be sources of wisdom, encouragement, and hope for the life of faith and the mission of discipleship in God's graced world.

NOTES

1. Karl Rahner, *Foundations of Christian Faith: An Introduction to the Idea of Christianity*, trans. William V. Dych (New York: Seabury, 1978), 51–54; original emphasis.

2. Nicholas Lash, *Holiness, Speech and Silence: Reflections on the Question of God* (Burlington, VT: Ashgate, 2004), 14.

3. Johann Baptist Metz, *Faith in History and Society: Toward a Practical Fundamental Theology*, rev. trans. J. Matthew Ashley (New York: Crossroad, 2007), 62.

4. Elizabeth A. Johnson, *She Who Is: The Mystery of God in Feminist Theological Discourse* (New York: Crossroad, 1993), 104.

5. Karl Rahner, "The Concept of Mystery in Catholic Theology," in *Theological Investigations*, vol. 4, trans. Kevin Smyth (New York: Crossroad, 1982), 57–58.

6. David Tracy, *Plurality and Ambiguity: Hermeneutics, Religion, Hope* (London: SCM, 1987), 73.

7. George P. Schner, "The Appeal to Experience," *Theological Studies* 53, no. 1 (1992): 54.

8. Schner, "Appeal to Experience," 54.

9. Rowan Williams, "Theological Integrity," *Cross Currents* 45 (1995): 323.

10. Vatican Council II, Dogmatic Constitution on Divine Revelation *Dei Verbum*, November 18, 1965, §2. Unless otherwise noted, all references to the documents of Vatican II are from *Vatican Council II: Constitutions Decrees Declarations*, rev. trans., ed. Austin Flannery (Collegeville, MN: Liturgical Press, 2014).

11. Francis, Encyclical on the Light of Faith, *Lumen fidei*, June 29, 2013, §35, http://www.vatican.va/content/francesco/en/encyclicals/documents/papa-francesco_20130629_enciclica-lumen-fidei.html.

12. Cynthia L. Rigby, "Knowing Our Limits and Laughing with Joy: Theology in Service to the Church Invisible," in *Theology in Service to the Church: Global and Ecumenical Perspectives*, ed. Alan Hugh Cole (Eugene, OR: Cascade Books, 2014), 107.

13. Francis, Encyclical on Fraternity and Social Friendship, *Fratelli tutti*, October 3, 2020, §55, http://www.vatican.va/content/francesco/en/encyclicals/documents/papa-francesco_20201003_enciclica-fratelli-tutti.html.

14. Constance Fitzgerald, "A Discipleship of Equals: Voices from Tradition—Teresa of Avila and John of the Cross," in *Desire, Darkness, and Hope: Theology in a Time of Impasse*, ed. Laurie Cassidy and M. Shawn Copeland (Collegeville, MN: Liturgical Press, 2021), 41.

15. Fitzgerald, "Discipleship of Equals," 41.

16. Francis, Encyclical on Care for Our Common Home, *Laudato si'*, May 24, 2015, §208, http://www.vatican.va/content/francesco/en/encyclicals/documents/papa-francesco_20150524_enciclica-laudato-si.html.

17. Vatican Council II, Pastoral Constitution on the Church in the Modern World, *Gaudium et spes*, December 7, 1965, §57, https://www.vatican.va/archive/hist_councils/ii_vatican_council/documents/vat-ii_const_19651207_gaudium-et-spes_en.html.

18. John Paul II, Encyclical on the Relationship between Faith and Reason, *Fides et ratio*, September 14, 1998, §43, https://www.vatican.va/content/john-paul-ii/en/encyclicals/documents/hf_jp-ii_enc_14091998_fides-et-ratio.html.

19. John Paul II, Apostolic Letter to the Bishops, Clergy, and Lay Faithful at the Close of the Great Jubilee of the Year 2000, *Novo millennio ineunte*, January 6, 2001, §52, https://www.vatican.va/content/john-paul-ii/en/apost_letters/2001/documents/hf_jp-ii_apl_20010106_novo-millennio-ineunte.html.

20. Karl Rahner, "The Eternal Significance of the Humanity of Jesus for Our Relationship with God," in *Theological Investigations*, vol. 3, trans. Karl-H. Kruger and Boniface Kruger (New York: Crossroad, 1982), 40.

21. Rahner, "Eternal Significance," 40.

22. For other instances of God's promise to be with God's people, see also Exod 6:7, Jer 30:22, and Ezek 36:28; the theme of God's everlasting commitment also appears at the end of the New Testament, see Rev 21:3.

23. On the meaning of the covenants between God and Israel, including their future orientation, see Andrew Davis, "A Biblical View of Covenants Old and New," *Theological Studies* 81, no. 3 (2020): 631–48.

24. Francis, Apostolic Exhortation on the Proclamation of the Gospel in Today's World, *Evangelii gaudium*, November 24, 2013, §3, http://www.vatican.va/content/francesco/en/apost_exhortations/documents/papa-francesco_esortazione-ap_20131124_evangelii-gaudium.html.

25. Daniel J. Harrington, *What Are We Hoping For? New Testament Images* (Collegeville, MN: Liturgical Press, 2006), vii.

26. Karl Rahner, *The Love of Jesus and the Love of Neighbor*, trans. Robert Barr (New York: Crossroad, 1983), 17; original emphasis.

27. Dermot Lane, *The Experience of God: An Invitation to Do Theology*, rev. ed. (Mahwah, NJ: Paulist Press, 2003), 21.

28. Francis, *Lumen fidei*, §39.

29. Vatican Council II, Decree on Priestly Training, *Optatam totius*, October 28, 1965, 16, https://www.vatican.va/archive/hist_councils/ii_vatican_council/documents/vat-ii_decree_19651028_optatam-totius_en.html.

Part Two

FOUNDATIONAL COMMITMENTS

4

THE HORIZON OF THEOLOGICAL EDUCATION

Formation in Faith

Thomas H. Groome

WE DON'T TYPICALLY think of formation in faith as integral to doing theology. Traditionally trained theologians tend to perceive the purpose of their discipline as the grounding and clarifying of theological ideas and beliefs, dogmas and doctrines. Formation in faith certainly draws upon theology but is more the responsibility of catechesis, be that in the home, a parish program, or Catholic school.

My proposal in this essay is that we resolutely come to understand and "do" theology in ways that are deeply formative of people's faith and spiritual lives. To neglect formation is to embrace the dominant epistemology of Western academia that narrows *knowing* to scientific data and rational ideas, with little care for formation of who people become.

To state the obvious, to reflect upon and speak of God (*theos logia*), and particularly of God as revealed in Jesus Christ, must surely demand that teaching and learning Christian theology be formative of people's lives in faith. For the God of Jesus, whom he had come to know first as Yahweh of his Jewish faith, clearly has very practical intentions for human history and for the lives of people within it. From the first call of Abraham and Sarah to parent a people uniquely God's own, down to God's work of liberating salvation in Jesus Christ, now continued by the Holy Spirit, it is clear that God intends all who embrace such faith to become and *live* as God's own people.

The intended "learning outcome," then, of doing Christian theology is to encourage *living* faith; by this I mean Christian faith that is *alive* and growing, *lived* in daily life, and *life-giving* for self, others, and the world. Jesus symbolized the horizon of such faith as the "reign of God"—God's best hopes for all humankind and all of creation. Further, Jesus ever emphasized that disciples are called to live into and work to realize God's reign "on earth as it is in heaven" (Matt 6:10)—now. Christian theology should serve such formative purpose. Indeed, to embrace faith in God as revealed in Jesus makes formation of people in *living* faith the ultimate purpose of all Christian theologizing.

I note parenthetically that when I refer to theological educators throughout this essay I primarily intend those who teach theology at a graduate and/or undergraduate level—the focus of this collection. However, the basic pedagogical proposals are also relevant for those who teach theology in Catholic high schools.

FOR REFLECTION

- What is your own sense of the nature and purpose of Christian theology?
- What might be required that theological education be formative in faith?

Ancient Wisdom to Retrieve

A frequent note in the writings of the renowned French Catholic scholar Jean-Luc Marion, is that epistemology is the gravest crisis facing the Western world today.[1] This is because we have greatly reduced knowing to technical rationality—what works for production—without any formative concern or ethical consideration. Given the many crises we face, Marion's claim may well sound exaggerated. Yet the negative potential of solely instrumental reasoning about empirical data, neglecting human experience and devoid of ethical concern, is surely writ large now in our destruction of the environment and has brought us to the brink of nuclear holocaust.

This is also evident in the dominant epistemology throughout American education—from kindergarten to research universities. Overall, that triumph of technical reasoning prioritizes the STEM courses (science, technology, engineering, and math). These are often portrayed as advancing people's "race to the top"—based on standardized testing—with no attention to ethical formation. Even the token civics curriculum has been largely abandoned in American public schools, as if people's social responsibilities are of no concern to education.

Of course we both need and benefit greatly from the STEM curriculum in our schools and the fruits of its ways of knowing (for example, the laptop on which I write). Likewise, there are many fine teachers who specialize in the scientific fields of study and yet are committed to teaching their students in formative and value-laden ways. Indeed, there are clarion voices of concern regarding the scientizing of American education who call loudly for a more humanizing approach, even a spiritually grounded one.[2] For its part, surely Catholic theology must reflect a holistic epistemology and provide education that is deeply formative.

Note well that Western epistemology was once much focused on formation; here we can only note a few highlights from a long-winded story. In the ancient intellectual traditions of Greece and Rome, the primary purpose of all education was to prepare people to be good citizens in the public realm. Formation in virtue was the primary intent of the Greek educational system of *paideia* and of the Roman *humanitas*. Plato was convinced that if you truly know "the good" you will do it, whereas for Aristotle, if you do the good, you will know it. Yet both were emphatic that education is an ontological affair, aimed at forming people's very *being* (the Greek *ontos*) as good citizens. For this reason, Plato and Aristotle typically wrote of education within the realm of politics, it being responsible for the formation of *polites*—citizens.

Aristotle did outline three ways of knowing as *theoria*, *praxis*, and *poiesis*, corresponding approximately to theoretical, practical, and aesthetic modes of cognition.[3] However, he saw all three as reliable and needed, as complementary, and with each contributing to the well-being of society. Western epistemology, however, from the Enlightenment movement onward (beginning around 1650) came to favor a more rationalist or *theory-to-practice* way of knowing, with the latter as applied theory rather than its own source of practical wisdom, and dismissing entirely the poetic/aesthetic as unreliable for "sure and certain ideas" (Descartes).

The implication, and especially for education, was to assume that knowing begins with the rational theoretical that is then to be applied, if it has any application, to practice. Note that in giving priority to theory, knowing came to privilege scholars and academia, dismissing the common-sense wisdom that ordinary people have from their life-praxis in the world, and with little attention to personal and ethical formation.

Many scholars would say that the later Enlightenment movement took this diminishment of knowing a step further, limiting knowledge to what arises from technical reasoning about empirical data.[4] Surely theological educators must resist such impoverished epistemology. To be faithful to its purpose of informing, forming, and transforming people toward *living* Christian faith, theology must honor all three ways of knowing—the theoretical, practical, and aesthetic—and not as sequential but as a perichoretic circle. Further, it must engage the whole person: head, heart, and hands—the *soul*—and be situated in time and place.

FOR REFLECTION

- What are the challenges in our post-modern world to a humanizing and formative theological education?
- What ways of knowing might respond to the challenges?

Signs and Seeds of Hope

Concerning epistemology, the poet William Butler Yeats once wrote wisely in "A Prayer for Old Age":

> God guard me from those thoughts men think
> In the mind alone;
> He that sings a lasting song
> Thinks in the marrow-bone.[5]

The epistemology of modernity limited knowing to "the mind alone" and, in fact, to "reason" alone, largely neglecting the mind's other two capacities—memory and imagination. An epistemology that encourages personal and ethical formation, however, must engage the "marrow bone" of people, their very souls, as they reflect upon and draw wisdom from the experiences of daily living. Likewise, it should engage people's *whole* mind, their reason indeed, and then their memory and imagination as well. As Augustine argued, all three are needed for knowing and are to function as a threesome, much like the Blessed Trinity.[6] To be formative, then, theological education must embrace a holistic epistemology, engaging people beyond a narrow rationalism toward spiritual wisdom for life.

Happily, many postmodern thought leaders, spurred on by people like Marion, Taylor, and Sandra Harding (emphasizing feminist ways of knowing),[7] are challenging and proposing alternatives to an epistemology of "the mind alone." We can also be encouraged toward a "marrow bone" alternative by a biblical epistemology; the Bible's overall intended "learning outcome" is spiritual wisdom for life that engages and shapes people's total *being*. I cite just one notable example.

John's Gospel has Jesus declare, "This is eternal life, that they may *know* you, the only true God, and Jesus Christ whom you have sent" (17:3; emphasis added). Clearly, the knowing referred here is far more than "knowing about" in an abstract or purely theoretical way. To "know" God and Jesus engages the whole person in spiritual wisdom that bears the promise of eternal life. It is significant, surely, that the verb for knowing here is the Greek *ginosko*, which also meant sexual intercourse (check Luke 1:34). And the same can be found of the Hebrew Scriptures with the verb *yada* meaning both to know and to make love. Clearly, the knowing intended by biblical faith, and thus for Christian theology, is to engage people's very *being* and every aspect of it—again, their "marrow bone."

There are also seeds of more holistic ways of knowing to be found and retrieved from the Catholic intellectual tradition. For example, Augustine was adamant that education must engage the soul of people, drawing out the wisdom "already within" them.[8] Thomas Aquinas was emphatic that all knowing begins with people's own sense experience and their reflection upon it; it was this insight of Aquinas that inspired the life-forming and participative pedagogies of both Maria Montessori and Paulo Freire. No one, however, has done more to retrieve a holistic way of knowing from the Catholic intellectual tradition than Bernard Lonergan (1904–1984).

Drawing especially upon Aquinas, Lonergan argued persuasively that "authentic cognition" (his term) demands a deliberate and fourfold dynamic, namely of *attending* to data (from both people's own lives in the world and from formal traditions of learning), of *understanding* the data, of making *judgments* about it, and finally of reaching *decisions*. So while Anselm defined *theology* as "faith seeking understanding," Lonergan would advise that "understanding" is only halfway toward the desired learning outcome. Our pedagogy must ever invite beyond *understanding* and encourage people to make *judgments* and *decisions* about what they know or are learning. Further, Lonergan persuasively argued that engaging the full dynamics of cognition is what leads people beyond knowledge toward wisdom for life *and* encourages their ethical formation.[9]

Note that the curriculum of much education, including theological, does not take seriously the *data* of people's lives in the world—what they can learn from their own historical praxis and aesthetic engagement (Aristotle's *praxis* and *poiesis*)—and focuses, instead, on imparting from scholarly traditions of learning (*theoria*). Then most teachers, even of theology, are typically satisfied by students coming to *understand* what is being taught and fail to invite them onward toward *judgments* and *decisions*; the latter two dynamics are key to spiritual and moral formation.

FOR REFLECTION

- Imagine a way of teaching theology that would be formative of people's lives.
- What would be some of its pedagogical moves and commitments?

An Intentional Pedagogy

For theological education to be formative, it must engage holistic ways of knowing and honor the dynamics of authentic cognition outlined above: *attending to* and *understanding* the data of both life-in-the-world *and* the discipline of theology, and then inviting people onward to *judgment* and *decision*. To realize such theological education in a classroom, so much depends on the pedagogy employed. To state the obvious, a purely didactic pedagogy is less likely to be formative than a participative one that engages all as active co-learners together.

Such a participatory pedagogy poses a huge challenge to all theological educators—including myself—because few of us have been taught theology by such a participatory pedagogy; the delivery lecture has been more our experience. Now, many doctoral dissertations in education have been written around the question "Why do teachers teach the way they teach?"; invariably, the finding is that "teachers tend to teach the way that they were taught." Breaking that pedagogical circle will require great intentionality on our part. Yet, I'll wager that all of us have had at least one good and formative theology teacher who inspired us to embrace this vocation; this is surely the one to emulate.

We can also draw upon the wisdom of great pedagogues, appropriating their insights into our own discipline and model of teaching. For the remainder of this essay, I will draw upon three of the greatest and my favored models, namely, John Dewey (1859–1952),[10] Maria Montessori (1870–1952),[11] and Paulo Freire (1921–1997).[12] Inspired by them, I propose ten pedagogical moves (some overlap) that a theological educator might employ toward a theology that is formative. While I lay them out here with some logical sequence, they are not to be followed lockstep; they are more like pedagogical commitments that a theology teacher might practice throughout any teaching/learning event, often repeating or renewing them as the event unfolds.

(1) *Establish the primary paradigm as conversation.* The dominant ethos of a formative theological pedagogy needs to be one of conversation, with the give and take that a good conversation entails and with all welcome to participate according to their learning style. Its etymology *con versare* implies to "turn around together," to mentor each other as co-learners. We need to encourage conversation within and between participants, with the educator, and engaging the texts and sources of Christian faith. The educator must prompt participants to share their own insights and wisdom (most often by posing good questions) and then ensuring that all are heard and taken seriously.

Let me clarify that an overall paradigm of conversation does not exclude lecturing that gives participants ready access to the data of tradition. As I elaborate below, lecturing can be crafted as more a conversation than a delivery, with the presenter building in examples and reflective questions, and accessing the relevant data as for consideration and appropriation by participants—rather than for acceptance and repeating.

(2) *Create a hospitable teaching/learning community.* Following on, the overall environment should be one where all participants feel welcome and included, respected and honored as agents of knowing in their own right. The ideal is that theological educators know their students' names and that students get to know each other's names. (A few times around the group in early classes can be effective, or name tags early on, and so on). Beyond their names, it helps the educator to know something of students' backgrounds and foregrounds—their hopes. (I have found an initial questionnaire—which I title "a little of my story"—most helpful.)

The key is that all feel welcome in the community and to participate in its conversation, bringing their own wisdom to the table. As Montessori would advise, the whole class environment should affirm all its members, disposing them to actively participate according to their learning style, and encouraging each one's own agency for knowing by "their life-force within (the soul) that sends the world forward."[13]

(3) *Foster people's interests and get them actively engaged in the teaching/learning dynamic.* Dewey was fond of saying that people learn little of significance to life unless they are *interested.* To this end, Freire would advise establishing a "generative theme" for the teaching/learning occasion, something of relevance to people's lives and that they can recognize from their own life-praxis. When Lonergan names the first step in knowing as to *attend* to data, the latter should include the knowing that people have from their own lives-in-the-world as well as the data of a tradition of learning—here theology.

Shirley and Hargraves propose that getting students actively *engaged* in the teaching/learning dynamic is key to formative education—of any kind. They helpfully review five ways to encourage engagement: (1) "intrinsic value," also meaning that students recognize what is being taught as worth learning; (2) "importance" in that students experience the curriculum as significant to their own lives; (3) "association" meaning that all students feel included and have a sense of belonging; (4) "empowerment" that gives students voice as real participants in the teaching/learning community; and (5) "mastery" in that they can experience a sense of accomplishment in what they learn.[14]

Theological education is certainly capable of such engagement by participants; we need to intentionally encourage as much!

(4) *To speak their own word and name their own reality*. Following on, and as Freire would emphasize, the pedagogy should deliberately encourage people to "speak their own word," to name their own *realidad*—how they perceive their praxis in the world around the generative theme of the occasion. He would also claim that such a pedagogical move—inviting people to their own voice—is the first step toward an emancipatory way of knowing, toward a liberating pedagogy. For Freire, the latter is the antithesis to "banking education," as in making deposits in passive receptacles.

(5) *Prompt critical reflection*. Here *critical* refers to discerning (rather than simply negative) and the *reflection* is to engage reason, memory, and imagination. Good theological education should surely prompt people to think for themselves in dialogue with each other and with the tradition to be taught. Critical discernment should also invite participants to recognize the influences of their sociocultural context on their own knowing and life-praxis.

In a sense this commitment is inviting people to think for themselves and then to think about their thinking, as in to recognize its contextual sources and historical influences. Likewise, the pedagogy should encourage students to *remember* what they already know from their life-in-the-world and to *imagine* life-giving possibilities for themselves and others.

(6) *Encourage contemplative reflection*. Here I'm inspired by Montessori's commitment to a contemplative way of knowing that encourages students to listen to that "life force within"—to their souls. This can encourage students in a deep listening to themselves and to the Holy Spirit at work within their hearts. It is interesting to note that for the first thousand years, Christian theology was largely a spiritual exercise of talking and listening to God, epitomized in the *lectio divina* of the monasteries. Then the next thousand years appealed more to reason, epitomized in theology as "queen of the sciences" within the universities. To form people in *living* faith, theology will do well to engage both the monastic and scholastic ways of knowing.

Why not build in moments of *lectio divina* or other forms of contemplation in a theology course? Why not have meditative pauses on the themes and topics being taught, making prayerful reflection as well as critical thinking integral to the overall pedagogy. Of course, we first need to be convinced that both are valid ways of knowing—particularly for theology.

(7) *Give persuasive access to the Story and Vision of Christian faith.* I use Story here as a metaphor of the whole corpus of Christian faith as represented in Scripture and Tradition. The Vision, then, entails all that the Story means for and asks of people's lives toward *living* faith—faith that is *alive, lived,* and *life-giving* for oneself, for others, and for the world. Our accessing of the Christian Story/Vision should be persuasive, proposing to participants how it has been life-giving across the ages and can still be so for our time. By way of pedagogy, "story" encourages accessing the faith tradition with narrative(s) as much as possible, rather than solely by abstract language patterns. The narrative is more likely to encourage personal engagement.

Accessing tradition can be done in many ways—studying required texts, personal or group research, collaborative partnerships, communication media, and so on. Often, however, it can be accessed most expeditiously by a lecture presentation (now with the help of slideshow presentations and the like). As suggested in the first pedagogical move above, a lecture/presentation can be crafted more as a conversation than a delivery, making proposals rather than proclamations, and by interspersing good reflective questions and examples throughout. A good lecture is one that stimulates people to think for themselves rather than telling them what to think.

(8) *Invite participants to personally appropriate their own knowing.* While appropriation should be encouraged throughout a teaching/learning event, it is well to have an intentional moment when participants are explicitly invited to discern their own emerging knowledge, to embrace as their own what is being accessed. This echoes Lonergan's emphasis on *judgment* as essential for authentic cognition. However, rather than our usual sense of "judgment," I think of this moment as participants discerning and appropriating as their own what is being taught, inviting them to "come to see" for themselves.

This pedagogical move amounts to inviting people to recognize their own emerging knowledge and what it could mean for their lives. It is an integrative move that can be as simple as asking participants, "So what is emerging for you now?" or "What are you coming to see for yourself?" or "What makes sense to you?" or "What do you agree with, disagree with, or add to what is emerging?" The undergirding pedagogy here is inviting participants to integrate what they know from reflecting on their own lives-in-the-world with what is presented as the faith tradition, encouraging them to appropriate the two sources into their own knowing.

(9) *Invite to personal decision.* Corresponding to Lonergan's fourth and final move in the dynamics of cognition and to be formative, every event should invite participants to *decide* what to "do" with their acquired insights and wisdom, how they might put them to work in their own lives of faith. This is most precisely how theological education can be formative. The decisions can be: *cognitive*—what they personally embrace with conviction; *emotive*—how they feel or might pray about it; or *behavioral*—how they might respond in their everyday lives. Or decisions may well be a combination of all three. And while we cannot grade people on their personal outcomes and convictions, we can well evaluate their *understanding* of what has been taught, the care with which they *appropriate* the content as their own, and the *responsibility* they take for their decisions.

(10) *Even formal lectures are to encourage personal engagement and responses.* Here I have in mind a formal lecture situation where the lecturer is expected to set forth a well-prepared paper or presentation; theology faculty often find themselves in such situations. The stereotypical way of conducting such an event is to begin with a formal introduction of the "speaker" (laudatory of their academic scholarship), followed by their presentation, and then, typically, what is designated as "questions and answers." The assumption that undergirds the stereotypical Q&A move is that the speaker has even more knowledge than already lectured, and is willing to give further answers to people's further questions.

But reflect on the pedagogical assumptions that undergird this typical pattern. It is as if the presenter has all the answers, and the participants only questions. Why not, after a presentation (or a pause in the midst of), give participants a few moments to reflect on and discern what they are hearing and how they are responding, what they recognize or are coming to see for themselves. Then, perhaps, give five minutes (or so) to "talk with a neighbor" to share their own wisdom in response to the presentation. After that, bring all back together and invite people to share their own thoughts and fresh insights. My own pattern here is to say something like, "of course I welcome your questions, but even more so your insights and wisdom." It invariably leads to a rich conversation rather than further lecturer monologue.

An Approach

As said at the outset, these ten aspects of a theological pedagogy for formation are general commitments to be realized throughout a theology course rather than sequential moves. So, while they begin by personally engaging people as active participants in the teaching/learning dynamic, we must maintain that engagement throughout the whole event or curriculum. While inviting people to think for themselves is listed as the third pedagogical move above, we must encourage them to do so throughout the whole process, and so on. So what I have proposed here is more a general pedagogical approach than a specific method. I'm confident that such a pedagogy will enhance the formative potential of theological education.[15]

FOR REFLECTION

- Reviewing these pedagogical moves, what might you adopt into your own approach?
- What other hard-won wisdom can you add to the pedagogy outlined above?

Encouraged by the Pedagogy of Jesus?

This closing reflection may seem like "loading the dice"—to pose Jesus as a model of a participatory and formative pedagogy. Yet, and though from a very different time and place, a brief review indicates that his pedagogy at least echoed much of what I propose above.

First, note that I have found very sparse scholarship on the actual pedagogy of Jesus; the books about *what* he taught could fill many libraries but there is comparatively little on *how* he taught. A notable exception is Pheme Perkins' small book *Jesus as Teacher*.[16] Here, also, we encounter the perennial debate regarding "the historical Jesus" and what we can attribute reliably to that Carpenter from Nazareth. Personally I find most helpful the moderating position of the renowned New Testament scholar José Pagola, who contends that the first Christian communities who were closest to Jesus and initiated the oral traditions and pericopes that later became the Gospels can lend us "a historical approximation" of him.[17] Within this approximation, I believe we can discern a reliable sense of *how* he taught. Let us briefly, then, review Jesus's pedagogy through the lens of the ten pedagogical moves outlined above.

Many times and from the beginning of Jesus's public ministry, the Gospels note the *inclusivity* of his table fellowship, including "sinners and tax collectors" (e.g., Mark 2:15–17). Such table fellowship epitomized his commitment to building up a *welcoming community* and likewise to a *mode of conversation*; what else do people do at a meal table? Jesus's commitment to conversation is also reflected in the many questions that he posed to people; scholars count over three hundred in the Gospels (though he answered only three himself).[18]

Jesus's pedagogy encouraged people's own *interests* and active *engagement* in many ways but particularly by turning them to some aspect of their own lives in the world. Here one thinks especially of the parables in the Synoptics (baking bread, sowing grain, sorting fish, hiring workers, etc.) and the metaphors and analogies we find in John (good shepherd, light of life, and others). By such turning people to their own everyday lives in the world, Jesus gained their immediate *interest* and actively *engaged* them with what he might have to say and was relevant to their context.

There are ample instances of Jesus encouraging and modeling *critical reflection*; for example, "you have heard it said, but I say…" (see Matt 5:17–47), or his many instances of suspending the law of Sabbath, for example, to cure a woman "bent over" (see Luke 13:10–17). However, his prompting of critical reflection seems most intense in his parables of reversal. So the prodigal is welcomed home, the Samaritan is the neighbor, Lazarus goes home to God, the widow's mite is most generous, and so on. These reversals would have turned people's taken-for-granted perspectives upside down, engaging them in deep discernment and leading them to question many of their sociocultural assumptions.

Likewise, much of Jesus's teaching was crafted as *contemplative*, be it his invitation to reflect on the birds of the air or the grain growing silently or the fresh buds emerging on the trees, and so on. And some thirty times the Gospels note him "going aside" to pray, and, of course, he taught his disciples to pray.

Then he certainly represented with *persuasion* his gospel of the reign of God, beginning with the launch of his public ministry, especially in Mark. This surely took great courage in the aftermath of John the Baptist being arrested (see Mark 1:14–15). Throughout his public teaching, Jesus boldly taught the great *Story* and *Vision* of God's reign, often favoring a *narrative* language pattern. Again, we can cite the analogy parables regarding the reign of God. And he encouraged those learned in God's reign to bring forth "from the treasury (of tradition) what is new and what is old" (see Matt 13:52)—accessing persuasively the greatest story ever told with an ever-unfolding vision.

Though the people readily recognized, and from the beginning, that Jesus "taught with authority" (see Mark 1:22), yet his pedagogy reflected a deep respect for people's own *discernment* and *decision*-making. His call to discipleship was ever by invitation, and with the right to refuse (which some did—see John 6:66; Matt 19:22, etc.). Jesus often blessed those who had the eyes to see and the ears to hear (Matt 13:16); clearly he meant more than physical sight and hearing. He ever wanted people to see and hear for themselves and then to *choose* to follow as disciples.

Jesus's engaging of people's lives, causing them to reflect, instructing them in his gospel, and inviting them to see for themselves, was sometimes hinted in just one verse. For example, "Look at the birds of the air [engaging]; they neither sow nor reap nor gather into barns [reflecting], and yet your heavenly Father feeds them [instruction]. Are you not of more value than they?" (*discernment* and *decision*) (Matt 6:26). Might we proceed somewhat similarly toward formative theological education?

FOR REFLECTION

- From the perspective of its pedagogy, read and reflect on the story of the Risen Christ accompanying two bewildered disciples on the Road to Emmaus (Luke 24:13–35). Note his deep engaging of them, his mode of instruction, his enabling them to "see for themselves" and make a decision to return to Jerusalem and to *living* faith.

NOTES

1. See, for example, *Givenness and Hermeneutics* (Milwaukee, WI: Marquette University Press, 2013).

2. See, for example, Nel Noddings, *The Challenge to Care in Schools: An Alternative Approach to Education* (New York: Teacher's College Press, 1992); Parker J. Palmer, *To Know as We Are Known: A Spirituality of Education* (San Francisco: Harper & Row, 1983); and a recent text from two renowned faculty at the Boston College School of Education and Human Development, Dennis Shirley and Andy Hargreaves, *Five Paths of Student Engagement: Blazing the Trail to Learning and Success* (Bloomington, IN: Solution Tree Press, 2021).

3. See Aristotle, *Nicomachean Ethics* (Cambridge, MA: Loeb Classical Library, 1982), esp. ch. 10.

4. See Charles Taylor, *A Secular Age* (Cambridge, MA: Harvard University Press, 2007), for a review of this history of epistemology and especially its implications for faith; the introduction offers a helpful summary.

5. William Butler Yeats, "A Prayer for Old Age," in *W. B. Yeats: Selected Poetry*, ed. A. Norman Jeffares (London: Macmillan, 1968), 175–76.

6. See Augustine of Hippo, *The Trinity*, in *The Fathers of the Church*, vol. 10 (Washington, DC: Catholic University of America Press), 311.

7. Sandra Harding, *Whose Science? Whose Knowledge?: Thinking from Women's Lives* (Ithaca, NY: Cornell University Press, 1991).

8. See, for example, Augustine, *The Teacher*, in *Ancient Christian Writers*, vol. 9 (New York: Newman Press, 1949), esp. chs. 11–14.

9. For a summary statement of Lonergan's dynamics of cognition, see his *Method in Theology* (New York: Seabury, 1972), esp. ch. 1.

10. I think of Dewey's *Experience and Education* (New York: Collier Books, 1938) as his briefest and most precise description of his favored pedagogy.

11. See Maria Montessori, *The Montessori Method* (New York: Schocken Books, 1969).

12. For his most precise statement, see Paulo Freire, *Pedagogy of the Oppressed* (New York: Seabury, 1970), esp. part 1.

13. Montessori, *Montessori Method*, 23.

14. See Shirley and Hargraves, *Five Paths of Student Engagement*, esp. chs. 1 and 6.

15. For a more complete statement of such a participatory pedagogy, see my *Will There Be Faith?: A New Vision for Educating*

and Growing Disciples (San Francisco: Harper One, 2011), esp. chs. 8 and 9.

16. Pheme Perkins, *Jesus as Teacher* (Cambridge: Cambridge University Press, 1990).

17. See José A. Pagola, *Jesus: An Historical Approximation* (Miami, FL: Convivium Press 2009).

18. See Martin B. Copenhaver, *Jesus Is the Question: The 307 Questions Jesus Asked and the 3 He Answered* (Nashville, TN: Abingdon Press, 2014).

5

THE PRIMACY OF CULTURAL CONTEXTUALITY

Hosffman Ospino

"AND THE WORD became flesh" (John 1:14). Enfleshed existence in the here and now of the always limited yet boundless human experience. Male, poor, Jewish. The adopted child of a carpenter. The firstborn son of Mary. A Galilean living under the rule of an expanding empire and at the crossroads of the Greco-Roman cultural world. The itinerant preacher whose "I am" confirmed to those who heard him that he was one of them, an "I am" that also evoked sacred words, a name divine: *ehyeh asher ehyeh* (I am who I am). Jesus of Nazareth. The teacher who made religious and political leaders uncomfortable while giving comfort to the poor and afflicted of his time. He prayed in Aramaic, shared parables in Hebrew, and rebuked Pontius Pilate in Latin. The fateful innocent who endured the punishment reserved for criminals and enemies by dying, alone and despised, on a cross on the outskirts of Jerusalem. Three days after his burial, his body was never found. A community of witnesses say that God brought him back from the dead. We believe their witness. We believe in him as the Savior and Redeemer. He is the Lord.

No theological effort attempting to understand the life, message, and meaning of Jesus of Nazareth, the Christ, can be deemed credible, relevant to the community of Christian believers and those who seek to know more about who he is, if it does not affirm the centrality of his enfleshed experience and historical existence. Everything about his life matters because each aspect of it reveals something about who he was in relationship to God and those with whom he partook. Likewise, no theological effort attempting to understand who Christians are, as we discern the life, message, and meaning of Jesus of Nazareth, the Christ, can be deemed credible or relevant if it does not affirm the centrality of our enfleshed experience and historical existence. Everything about our lives matters because each aspect in them reveals something about who we are in relationship to God and those with whom we partake. Theological education that is authentically formative must locate itself at the intersection of these two convictions.

Cultural Selves

There is no such thing as a cultureless person or a culturally neutral existence.[1] Any attempt to claim that one is above, beyond, or without culture warrants close scrutiny. Much of what passes as education in Western societies, whether at the elementary school level or in the highly specialized world of higher education, tends to treat cultural particularity as an addendum, something ancillary, a set of categories that can be left at the door when education happens, perhaps a burden to be alleviated or a stain that needs purification. Such is the self-afforded dispensation of many who feel free to ignore the cultural rootedness of human existence, usually from a perspective of power and privilege, often assuming that their ways of life—also cultural—and their interpretations of reality—as culturally biased as anything else—are normative for all.

I do, research, teach, and write theology as a Hispanic man living in the United States. Much of the theological education work I do happens in the context of the graduate classroom in a Catholic university as part of my vocation to accompany theological scholars and ministers in their formation. I also do a significant amount of theological education while leading formation experiences with church leaders and people in faith communities, including my own parish where I have been involved for more than two decades. Almost invariably, Asian, Black, Hispanic, and other theologians from minoritized communities disclose our cultural rootedness and the "place" where we stand as we write and teach.[2] In doing so, we echo the wisdom and courage of many women theologians who insist that naming the particular experience of being a woman here and now matters when theologizing or educating theologically.

Our students and the faith communities where they come from, or those they plan on serving, must regularly endure the arbitrary racial and cultural taxonomies that U.S. society imposes through its legal, political, and economic systems upon everyone living in its territories, making cultural and racial identification unavoidable—unless one manages to pass as white.[3] Students from other nations and cultures who come to study in our seminaries, theologates, and universities find themselves at odds figuring out where they fit in that strange order. We speak of faith communities using labels such as "the Black parish" or "the Hispanic church." In the attempt to name who these groups are, willingly or unwillingly, in the larger universe of racial and cultural classifications, those labels scream loudly who they are not: white—or whichever other group considered dominant at any given time. Our theological schools and church structures parcel out our students according to similar categories. Groups form in light of their particularities; recruitment aims at meeting minimum quotas; accrediting agencies and supporters give us high marks if we meet their diversity standards.

Have you wondered why it is commonplace, almost expected, even if one resists that expectation, for theological educators and students from minoritized communities to make our presence and contributions known while naming our racial and cultural rootedness? I have pondered this question endlessly, returning always to a similar conclusion: we have no option. Asian, Black, and Brown bodies cannot hide. Neither do white bodies, ironically, and yet it is of the former that cultural self-disclosure is expected. Our enfleshed and culturally informed existence meets every day the constructs that society imposes to interpret such particular ways of being, placing us in different, sometimes awkward positions as we relate to one another. In the theological educational experience we meet as embodied beings engaged in faith-seeking understanding. That enfleshed existence, that being Asian, Black, Brown, and white, shapes how we teach, learn, and do theology. The cultural worlds we inhabit, named and unnamed, are the matrixes through which we make meaning about the divine, the world, others, and ourselves.[4]

Reflecting on the cultural diversity that shapes our contemporary world, Jacques Audinet observes,

> The entire world is in my street, in my city, and every big city....In the space of a few seconds people pass by whose gait, physical features, skin color, language, gestures, and behavior display a wide variety. As in a kaleidoscope, forms and colors are constantly transformed. Thanks to the present minglings and mergings, humanity has never been in a better position to fully recognize its extreme diversity.[5]

We can say likewise about the spaces where we form people theologically today in the United States. The entire world is in my theology class. If this is not happening yet in your institution or your faith community, it will, in time, unless you resist it or simply choose to isolate. Audinet anticipates a category that encapsulates the context that defines who we are as a human race, and one that holds potential to reimagine theological formation in the twenty-first century: *mestizaje*.

Mestizaje points to the experience of endless intermixing of races, cultures, and experiences that has shaped the human experience for millennia.[6] The term evokes a sense of "inescapability."[7] We all, without exception, carry the seeds of many cultures, races, and experiences in our genetic code, biologically and culturally. The myth of purity, whether racial or cultural is just that, a myth. *Mestizaje* points to a future, a dream of a humanity birthed into a common vision that fuses who we are with what we can become, preserving certain elements of the present and embracing the unpredictability of the unknown.[8] Such a dream demands awareness about tensions among differences, social disparities, power imbalances, hegemonic tendencies, movements of resistance, memories of violence, and ultimately the pervasive presence of sin. As such, between what is and what it can be, *mestizaje* is an affirmation of the human condition as it longs for life, justice, and restoration. *Mestizaje* emerges as a metaphor for life-giving grace. The thought is utopian—understanding utopia as *eu-topia*, "the place of the good,"[9] a vision that drives life commitments and aspirations.

From this vantage point, fresher approaches and pedagogies for theological education can emerge in our day. If we are going to speak of the formative character of theological education in our day, we must acknowledge that we all can learn much from those theological scholars, educators, and students who find ourselves naming our cultural and racial location, intentionally or forced by circumstances, as integral to the theological educational experience. *Mestizaje*, asserts Audinet, "carries a meaning for all humanity."[10] So does naming our racial and cultural rootedness. Roberto Goizueta speaks of the ambivalence of naming such situatedness:

> It is our very identity as mestizos/as and exiles, a people living in between, that, indeed, makes us ultimately unacceptable to the dominant U.S. culture. For that culture cannot accept what is "in between," what is "both/and"; it is a culture whose reality is comprised of oppositions and dichotomies. In a world of dichotomies, in a world of black or white, the mestizo/a can only be a nobody, since the mestizo/a cannot, by definition, fit within those categories. The mestizo/a and exile is a person who, by definition, inhabits the in-between world of "both/and." Indeed, this world is more than a habitat, it is our very identity.[11]

Cultural and racial situatedness is a *locus theologicus* within which we can learn much about how God becomes present in history and how we learn more about our humanity. In the context of theological education in a diverse and globalized world, I argue, naming cultural and racial situatedness is a *sine qua non locus formationis* (indispensable space of formation).

Contextual Existence

The naming of ones' cultural and racial particularity when engaging in instances of theological education is both an exercise of personal and communal self-disclosure. It is an invitation into a world of possibility. Such naming is also an exercise of epistemological honesty and humility that reveals the biases—positive and negative—that we bring into theologically formative processes.

We are. We are here and now. We are here and now, with others. We are here and now, with others whose lives unfold in the particularity of contextual existence. These four affirmations go hand in hand. Each is a proclamation, a manifesto that calls for an examination of pedagogical assumptions and a critical analysis of how theological education happens in our institutions, including the resources that we use for this task.

WE ARE

The cultural self, that is every human being, cries out, "*I am*," "*we are*." It is a declaration of existence, a call for recognition, an invitation into contemplating the *Imago Dei* imprinted in our enfleshed existences. In our increasingly diverse and globalized world, theological educators hear voices that for long were silenced, oppressed, and ignored, saying, sometimes out loudly, sometimes with timid reverberations, "*we are*." We hear voices that have enjoyed privilege for long and find themselves reckoning with the implications of such privilege, "becoming undone."[12] We still hear many voices that seemingly remain dissonant in contemporary conversations about diversity and inclusion, yet tacitly seek attention in a world in which the politics of recognition[13] shape much of our interaction as citizens and disciples. All these voices *are*. Every one of these voices are necessary to build a formative theological education community. Educational theorist bell hooks affirms that we build community by "[recognizing] the value of each individual voice."[14] In the theological education community gathered in the classroom or the church, at the pulpit, the street, or the field, sincerely listening to each individual voice demands assessing how and what we teach. We need to listen to those "I am" and "we are" in our midst:

> *I am the Brown Church*
> God calls me mija/mijo
> Brown, black, white, even yellow, are all within me
> When Black and White come to talk, my voice is not heard,
> I am not invited to the table
> I share much with my Black sisters and brothers, yet my voice is distinct
> I long, I cry out to be heard for who I am
> THE BROWN CHURCH.[15]

WE ARE HERE AND NOW

The shift to a historical consciousness[16] in the way Catholics theologize also has—or should have—major implications for the way in which we form others theologically. The Second Vatican Council in particular embraced such historical consciousness in its invitation to engage the realities of the world, *de facto* moving beyond a cosmological paradigm that treated the church as an institution and the community of the baptized as if existing in a different realm. We all are the church; we all live in the world. The opening words of *Gaudium et spes* are programmatic not only for the church's evangelizing mission today, but also for how we educate theologically: "The joys and the hopes, the griefs and the anxieties of the men of this age, especially those who are poor or in any way afflicted, these are the joys and hopes, the griefs and anxieties of the followers of Christ."[17]

To be formative, theological education, almost of necessity, must foster an awareness of the historical realities of our day and those of the past that have overwhelmingly affected minoritized communities (such as violence, racism, colonialism, sexism, etc.). Not doing this fostering of awareness may render the entire theological educational task irrelevant, even becoming a perpetuating force at the service of injustice under the guise of passing on the tradition in apolitical ways. When taking diversity and contextuality seriously, theological education needs to be political. Historical awareness demands theological education to form ministers and scholars, individuals and communities as active agents of history. Christians have a moral obligation to read and unread, interpret and reinterpret, construct and deconstruct history with a critical eye informed by the gospel, and theological education must prepare us to do this well.

Gaudium et spes also brings attention to the powerful notion of reading the signs of the times: "The Church has always had the duty of scrutinizing the signs of the times and of interpreting them in the light of the Gospel."[18] It may be tempting to read the category "signs of the times" as only spiritual signs of God's presence in the everyday. The bishops from Latin America who gathered in Medellín in 1968 ensured that this category would be understood also from prophetic and sociohistorical perspectives. The signs of the times, according to Medellín, are profoundly embedded in the social and political structures that shape the lives of the Christian community—and others. For Medellín, and echoed by subsequent CELAM (Consejo Episcopal Latinoamericano) general conferences, a most powerful sign of the times in our midst are the poor and the oppressed. Their presence and their cries rise to heaven while compelling the Christian community to respond to their plight and do something to address the causes of poverty and injustice.[19]

The reading and interpretation of the signs of the times can only happen within the horizon of a conversion of the heart: "for our true liberation to happen, all of us need a profound conversion so the 'Reign of justice, love and peace' may come to us....We will not have a new continent without new and reformed structures; actually, a new continent will not be possible without new people."[20] The transformation of structures will not happen without a true transformation of the heart. Theological education actualizes its formative nature when it prepares ministers and scholars to read the signs of the times prophetically and embark on a path to conversion.

WE ARE HERE AND NOW, WITH OTHERS

More than merely serving the marketplace demands of a random body of individuals seeking to grow in their faith, satisfy their intellectual curiosity, procure an academic credential, or discern some form of personal vocation, theological education that is formative emerges as an inherently communal enterprise. Formative theological education does all of the above, yet it does so while placing the value of communal existence at the center. Communality makes tangible the ecclesial character of theological education.[21]

Every person who participates in the theological formation experience—student, educator, administrator, community, supporter—is a vessel full of a priori communal wisdom that reflects the influence of a lifetime of multiple networks of relationships. We belong to families, faith communities, groups of mutual interest, guilds, educational legacies, neighborhoods, cities or towns, cultural worlds, racial and ethnic groups, and others. We discern with them what it means to believe. In time, the influence of each of these communal relationships, positive and negative, become part of who we are. We carry them with us. They do not stay at the classroom door or outside any other spaces where theological education occurs. They are us and we are them. The encounter of a group of persons in any exercise of theological education is the encounter of communities, memories, values, stories, and feelings.

When the theological educator or the theology or ministry student withholds their own voice or are rendered silent, those communal voices are also silenced. When the theological educator or the theology or ministry student speaks, they speak—and loudly. The sound of those individual and communal voices may fluctuate between the harmonious and the cacophonous, searching for meanings, seeking to create something new. This is why theological education, particularly amidst the cultural diversity that defines the Christian experience in the United States needs, as José Irizarry suggests, aesthetic spaces, "locations where the utopian possibilities that find restriction within the current social and cultural conditions can be rehearsed and practiced. An aesthetic space serves as a restricted space where people bring memory and imagination to make things possible here and now."[22]

Being here and now, with others, makes us accountable to the particular communities where we belong and to those we conceive through shared imagination. It seems imperative to assess to what extent such accountability remains a central aspect of our theological education initiatives. The theological education experience often prepares women and men for ministry and for a life of scholarly activity. Theological education programs in universities and seminaries, especially at the graduate level, by design use extraction models in which most faculty and students remove ourselves, literally, from our communities to join self-contained and somewhat artificial educational enclaves. While the practice is conducive to focusing time and energy on scholarly activities, we must ask to what extent regular contact with the everyday experience of faith communities factors into the theological formation experience.

This is a great opportunity to ask some important questions: Where do we do our best theology? For whom do we write? What questions drive our theological education commitments? How often do we as theological educators "descend" from our intellectual and institutional echelons to touch base with the faith communities that eventually will welcome the ministers, leaders, and theological scholars we are training? For theological education to be authentically formative, it needs to cultivate a special closeness with the grassroots. Theologian Ada María Isasi-Díaz saw herself as an organic intellectual, drawing philosophical and theological insight from *lo cotidiano*, the everyday, along with other Hispanic women, especially those whose lives are shaped by daily struggle (*la lucha diaria*).[23] María Pilar Aquino, reflecting on the identity of the U.S. Hispanic Catholic theologian, elaborates further: "U.S. Latino/a theological reflection, then, starts from the lived faith of the community, which welcomes God's presence in its midst; celebrates it in its popular rituals, ceremonies, and prayers; and witnesses to it through the community's words and deeds."[24] The source and locus of theology as described by Isasi-Díaz and Aquino cannot be any different for theological education. That seems to be at the heart of Pope Francis's advice:

> Do not settle for a desktop theology. Your place for reflection is the frontier. Do not fall into the temptation to embellish, to add fragrance, to adjust them to some degree and domesticate them. Even good theologians, like good shepherds, have the odour of the people and of the street and, by their reflection, pour oil and wine onto the wounds of mankind.[25]

WE ARE HERE AND NOW, WITH OTHERS WHOSE LIVES UNFOLD IN THE PARTICULARITY OF CONTEXTUAL EXISTENCE

Theological educators today are more at home with the conviction that "any theology needs to attend both to its contextual and universalizing dimensions," as Robert Schreiter suggests.[26] This has not always been the case. In fact, there are still corners within Catholicism and other Christian traditions where the idea of attending to context is resisted—implicitly or explicitly—in favor of somewhat neutral, abstract, and ahistorical forms of theological reflection. Theological education practices grow in their embrace of contextuality. Forming the minds and hearts of ministers, leaders, and theological scholars to engage our culturally diverse and globalized world requires such an embrace.

Attention to contextuality in theological education implies much more than peppering our curriculum, syllabi, and pedagogies with authors, texts, and categories deemed "contextual"—meaning neither European, nor Euro-American, nor white nor male nor clerical, or any combination of these—while the core of the educational experience continues to reflect traditionally predominant voices and methodologies. There is still too much of what Marcella Althaus-Reid called a "theme park theologies" perspective in our theological education circles.[27] Although there is widespread acknowledgment of the theological contributions of historically marginalized and underrepresented communities, they are expected to accommodate to the standard intellectual and institutional presuppositions within which they are received and thus are treated as "theological subthemes worthy of being visited, and people in the West are encouraged to visit them as if going to a botanical garden."[28]

The situation is exacerbated in increasingly diverse classrooms and settings where students whose racial/cultural identity does not necessarily mirror that of the predominant groups that define the contours of the theological education experience, sometimes resisting conforming and simulation,[29] must nevertheless study theology often as passive recipients of traditions and interpretations of a Christian experience not their own. Such education occurs at the expense of their own voices and that of the communities from which they come and to which they are accountable. The following observation from Kwok Pui-lan should give us pause: "In a traditional and Eurocentric theology class, the experiences of international students and racial and ethnic minorities do not count much, and they are not seen as capable of producing knowledge."[30]

Conclusion

In order to be *formative*, theological education needs to take risks. In increasingly diverse churches and societies, and mindful of the effects of globalization, theological education must dare to form, reform, create, construct, beget, imagine. Allow me to conclude with three ways forward.

One, we must invest in practices of renewed awareness about cultural and racial/ethnic difference so theological educators and institutions can evaluate periodically our pedagogical commitments. Race matters; so does culture and context. Unchecked practices of theological education that get away with minimizing or ignoring the centrality of race, culture, and context in the lives of those we educate and the faith communities we serve risk becoming instruments of oppression and injustice.

Two, we need models of theological education that prophetically and courageously decenter predominant perspectives, without eliminating them, yet creatively integrate these and others into new ways of being community in context, fruit of an exercise of perennial becoming in the particularity of history.

Three, theological education in a world in which students of theology are more at home acknowledging how cultural, racial, and contextual situatedness define our relationships in church and society must aim at cultivating real intercultural competencies. When speaking of intercultural competencies, we could use as a starting point the definition the Catholic bishops of the United States use to guide ministerial formation: "*Intercultural competence* is the capacity to communicate, relate, and work across cultural boundaries. It involves developing capacity in three areas: *knowledge*, *skills*, and *attitudes*."[31]

A commitment to theological education that forms interculturally competent ministers, leaders, and scholars must be rooted in a clear embrace of the human person as a cultural self and a respectful awareness of contextual existence. Just as theological reflection must constantly contend with the inevitability of that event that redefined history, "And the Word became flesh," theological education that is formative must heed the voices of those who participate in its processes saying, we are…we are here and now…we are here and now, with others…we are here and now, with others whose lives unfold in the particularity of contextual existence.

NOTES

1. See Hosffman Ospino, "Foundations for an Intercultural Philosophy of Christian Education," *Religious Education* 104, no. 3 (2009): 303–14.

2. The bibliography is abundant. See, for instance, Sang Hyun Lee, *From a Liminal Place: An Asian American Theology* (Minneapolis: Fortress Press, 2010); Fernando F. Segovia and Mary Ann Tolbert, eds., *Reading from This Place*, vol. 1, *Social Location and Biblical Interpretation in the United States* (Minneapolis: Fortress Press, 1995).

3. See Ian Haney López, *White by Law: The Legal Construction of Race* (New York: New York University Press, 2006); Richard Rothstein, *The Color of Law: A Forgotten History of How Our Government Segregated America* (New York: Liveright Publishing Corporation / Norton, 2018).

4. See Hosffman Ospino, *Interculturalism and Catechesis: A Catechist's Guide to Responding to Cultural Diversity* (New London, CT: Twenty-Third Publications, 2017), 28.

5. Jacques Audinet, *The Human Face of Globalization: From Multicultural to Mestizaje* (Lanham, MD: Rowman & Littlefield, 2004), 7.

6. See Audinet, *Human Face of Globalization*, 35–62. For a thorough analysis of the use of *mestizaje* among Latino/a Catholic theologians as well as some important critiques, see Néstor Medina, *Mestizaje: (Re)Mapping Race, Culture, and Faith in Latina/o Catholicism* (Maryknoll, NY: Orbis Books, 2009).

7. See Audinet, *Human Face of Globalization*, 48.

8. See Audinet, *Human Face of Globalization*, 128–41.

9. See Jon Sobrino, *No Salvation Outside the Poor: Prophetic-Utopian Essays* (Maryknoll, NY: Orbis Books, 2008), 80–82.

10. Audinet, *Human Face of Globalization*, 143.

11. Roberto S. Goizueta, *Caminemos con Jesús: Toward a Hispanic/Latino Theology of Accompaniment* (Maryknoll, NY: Orbis Books, 1995), 16–17.

12. See Keri Day, *Notes of a Native Daughter: Testifying in Theological Education* (Grand Rapids, MI: Eerdmans, 2021), 104–10.

13. See Charles Taylor, "The Politics of Recognition," in *Multiculturalism: Examining the Politics of Recognition*, ed. Amy Gutmann (Princeton, NJ: Princeton University Press, 1992), 25–73.

14. bell hooks, *Teaching to Transgress: Education as the Practice of Freedom* (New York: Routledge, 1994), 40.

15. Chao Romero, *Brown Church: Five Centuries of Latina/o Social Justice, Theology, and Identity* (Downers Grove, IL: IVP, 2020), 25. The words *mija/mijo* in English mean "daughter/son." Italics and capitals are original.

16. Bernard J. F. Lonergan, "The Transition from a Classicist Worldview to Historical Mindedness," in *Collected Works of Bernard Lonergan*, vol. 13, *A Second Collection*, ed. Robert M. Doran and John D. Dadosky (Toronto: University of Toronto Press, 2017), 3–10.

17. Vatican Council II, Pastoral Constitution on the Church in the Modern World, *Gaudium et spes*, December 7, 1965, §1, https://www.vatican.va/archive/hist_councils/ii_vatican_council/documents/vat-ii_const_19651207_gaudium-et-spes_en.html.

18. *Gaudium et spes*, §4.

19. See Consejo Episcopal Latinoamericano, *Medellín, Conclusions of the Second General Conference of Latin American Bishops* (Bogotá, Colombia: General Secretariat of CELAM), *Medellín*, Introduction, 4 and 5; Justice, 1. For a more detailed analysis of the theological category "signs of the times" in the general conferences sponsored by CELAM during the last half century, see Patricio Merino, "La categoría teológica signos de los tiempos en las Conferencias Generales del Episcopado Latinoamericano," in *Nuevos signos de los tiempos: Diálogo teológico íbero-latino-americano*, ed. Luis Aranguren Gonzalo and Félix Palazzi (Madrid: San Pablo, 2018), 28–39.

20. *Medellín*, Justice, no. 1. Author's translation.

21. This observation introduces a necessary differentiation between theological education as an ecclesial activity, meaning an intentional pursuit done by and on behalf of the community of the baptized, the people of God, and the mere study of religion as a phenomenon.

22. José R. Irizarry, "Toward an Intercultural Approach to Theological Education for Ministry," in *Shaping Beloved Community: Multicultural Theological Education*, ed. David V. Esterline and Ogbu U. Kalu (Louisville, KY: Westminster John Knox, 2006), 38. Irizarry borrows the category "aesthetic spaces" from Brazilian dramatist Augusto Boas.

23. Ada María Isasi-Díaz, "Lo Cotidiano: A Key Element of Mujerista Theology," *Journal of Hispanic / Latino Theology* 10, no. 1 (August 2002): 10.

24. María Pilar Aquino, "Theological Method in U.S. Latino/a Theology: Toward and Intercultural Theology for the Third Millennium," in *From the Heart of Our People: Latino/a Explorations in Catholic Systematic Theology*, ed. Orlando O. Espín and Miguel H. Díaz (Maryknoll, NY: Orbis Books, 1999), 25.

25. Francis, Letter of His Holiness Pope Francis to the Grand Chancellor of the "Pontificia Universidad Católica Argentina" for the 100th Anniversary of the Founding of the Faculty of Theology, March 3, 2015, https://www.vatican.va/content/francesco/en/letters/2015/documents/papa-francesco_20150303_lettera-universita-cattolica-argentina.html.

26. Robert J. Schreiter, *The New Catholicity: Theology between the Global and the Local* (Maryknoll, NY: Orbis Books, 1997), 3.

27. Marcella María Althaus-Reid, "Gustavo Gutiérrez Goes to Disneyland: *Theme Park Theologies* and the Diaspora of the Discourse of the Popular Theologian in Liberation Theology," in *Interpreting Beyond Borders*, ed. Fernando F. Segovia (Sheffield: Sheffield Academic Press, 2000), 36–58.

28. Althaus-Reid, "Gustavo Gutiérrez," 42.

29. On "simulation," see Althaus-Reid, "Gustavo Gutiérrez," 41.

30. Kwok Pui-lan, "Teaching Theology from a Global Perspective," in *Teaching Global Theologies: Power and Praxis*, ed. Kwok Pui-lan, Cecilia González-Andrieu, and Dwight N. Hopkins (Waco, TX: Baylor University Press, 2015), 26.

31. United States Conference of Catholic Bishops, Secretariat for Cultural Diversity in the Church, *Building Intercultural Competence for Ministers: Modules for Training Workshop*, bilingual ed. (Washington, DC: United States Conference of Catholic Bishops, 2014), 9.

6

EDUCATING IN A WAY OF JUSTICE

Nancy Pineda-Madrid

EVERY AGE HAS its own affronts to human dignity and a just life. Indeed, ours has seen a pandemic, the mortal assault on young Black and Brown lives, the degradation of our common home, planet earth, among many others. Because the principle of justice is foundational to formative theological education, it cannot be developed but through the idiom of justice. Indeed, any attempt to ignore the integral nature of the principle and practice of justice in formative theological education results in acute distortion, severely compromising its integrity. To say that justice is foundational means that justice is intrinsic to all that is formative theological education from its inception and beyond; and, that a commitment to justice guides every endeavor and aspect of what is formative theological education.

Justice is—according to Pope Francis in his 2020 encyclical letter *Fratelli tutti*—"to give to each his own…[which] means that no human individual or group can consider itself absolute, entitled to bypass the dignity and the rights of other individuals or their social groupings."[1] Notably, "justice requires recognizing and respecting not only the rights of individuals, but also social rights and the rights of peoples. This means finding a way to ensure 'the fundamental right of peoples to subsistence and progress.'"[2] This approach to justice requires a creative vigilance. As faithful believers committed to, as Pope Francis urges,

> The great principle that there are rights born of our inalienable human dignity, we can rise to the challenge of envisaging a new humanity. We can aspire to a world that provides land, housing and work for all....[To be sure,] a real and lasting peace will only be possible "on the basis of a global ethic of solidarity and cooperation in the service of a future shaped by interdependence and shared responsibility in the whole human family."[3]

Formative theological education grows from the soil of this commitment.

Formative theological education's commitment to justice finds its footing in a theological anthropology that cherishes the communal. To be sure, a communal theological anthropology offers a most compelling foundation for formative theological education precisely because it foregrounds human interrelatedness with all other human beings as constitutive of the God-human relationship. What is more, a communal theological anthropology encourages the cultivation of *reverence*, reverence for God, reverence for every other human life, and reverence for the whole of the created order. Paul Woodruff writes, "Reverence begins in a deep understanding of human limitations; from this grows the capacity to be in awe of whatever we believe lies outside our control—God, truth, justice, nature, even death. The capacity for awe, as it grows, brings with it the capacity for respecting fellow human beings, flaws and all."[4] A communal theological anthropology invites an interrogation of the degree to which we reverence the humanity of the "other," and in particular, the humanity of the most marginalized others. It concerns itself with how humans relate to one another and calls attention to how humans establish relationships with all that is. By foregrounding our interrelatedness with one another, a communal theological anthropology elicits within students, at a minimum, a heightened interest in justice, if not a growing, ardent commitment to the work of justice in the world.

A communal theological anthropology needs to be intentionally embraced, and thoughtfully cultivated. This intentionality is necessary due, in large part, to the overwhelming reign of individualism, something that repeatedly undermines the humanity of, and reverence for, others. This chapter begins by clarifying what a communal theological anthropology is and intends. Much flows from this commitment. The remaining two sections of the chapter explore emerging themes that flow from it, namely a praxis of solidarity grounded in commitment to the common good and ongoing openness to conversion, not only a conversion of the mind but of the heart as well.

A Communal Theological Anthropology

Intentionally embracing a communal theological anthropology is no easy task. Today, the prevailing anthropological understanding in the United States is shaped by what theologian John Markey calls hyper-individualism,[5] something Roberto Goizueta, also a theologian, frames as a "tradition of modern liberal individualism."[6] This understanding of the human person presumes a self that is "socially unsituated," meaning that individual human beings are understood to fundamentally exist *prior to* any relationships with other human beings. Thus, each individual human may choose to enter into a given relationship with others or not:

> Relationality is thus not essential to the individual person, but only a secondary, optional choice available to each person: I remain a complete person whether or not I choose to enter into relationships with others. Furthermore, since each individual is an essentially self-enclosed entity with no intrinsic relationship to others, there is no necessary relationship between one individual's life, or experience, and that of another individual: my experience is only mine, and yours is only yours.[7]

This kind of individualism has influenced theological anthropologies, despite the fact that it presents a severely distorted conception of the God-human relationship. This prevailing perception tends toward a presumption that our political, religious, and economic lives in society are composed of a collection of individual choices. Accordingly, individual rights are seen as foremost and sacred in the face of the state and all groupings of people, including ecclesial communities. With roots in the Enlightenment, individual rights are perceived to be "over against the state, the church, and all other collective entities," entities that are considered to pose "threats to individual autonomy."[8] Groups or communities within society are likewise presumed to be a collection of individuals, connected together in a temporary and voluntary way. The origins of this understanding of the human person are centuries old, making this understanding difficult to identify and analyze. Individualism is the air we breathe on a daily basis, and, like fish in water, it is difficult to be critically aware of what is a dominant mindset all around us.

Yet, this understanding of the human person effectively undermines and corrodes inclinations toward justice. Why? Because an individualist anthropology marginalizes and minimizes the importance of relationships, and it fails to see that the work of justice is fundamentally the pursuit of right relationships. In the face of an individualistic anthropology, the challenge to recognize and develop right relationships with one another in community is deemed to be, at best, unimportant, if not altogether nonsensical. Indeed, as Goizueta clarifies:

> Both the modern liberal individual and the totalitarian dictator view persons as autonomous individuals. The only difference is that the former celebrates the individual, while the latter fears him or her. As Alasdair MacIntyre contends, "the essence of individualism is not so much to emphasize the individual rather than the collective…as to frame all questions according to an ostensible antithesis between the individual and the collective."[9]

Thus, commitment to justice requires a communal theological anthropology, one that foregrounds relationality and summons persons to meet the challenge of right relationships. And inviting students to imagine and internalize a communal theological anthropology is a monumental task, one that requires swimming against the much stronger, pervasive current of individualism.

In broad strokes, a communal theological anthropology is reinforced when teaching foregrounds the trinitarian God. Since human beings are created in the image and likeness of God and the trinitarian God underscores the relationality of God, then, accordingly, human beings as *imago Dei* are ideally relational and/or social.[10] And, when teaching ecclesiology foregrounds the church as the Body of Christ, this too emphasizes the interrelatedness of human beings.[11] In the field of theological ethics, Catholic Social Teaching—the church's teaching on social, economic, political, and cultural matters—repeatedly underscores a communal theological anthropology through its many principles: the common good, the preferential option for the poor, solidarity, stewardship, and care for creation, to mention a few.[12]

In addition to these thematic considerations, among others, a communal theological anthropology is implied, and, at times, explicitly developed, in the many distinct forms of liberation theology. Given that liberation theologies further emancipation from oppression caused by classism, racism, sexism, and heterosexism, accordingly, they urge readers to take human interrelatedness as fundamental to what it means to be human. Indeed, the preferential option for the poor in Latin American liberation theologies has no meaning but for a communal theological anthropology. Black and womanist theologies denounce the sin of racism and sexism by standing grounded in a communal theological anthropology.[13] Feminist theologies advance a critique of sexism and queer theologies advance a critique of heterosexism both informed by a communal theological anthropology.[14] Each of these discourses—by virtue of their foregrounding of a population that suffers systemic oppression—presumes a communal theological anthropology.

While any one of these aforementioned discourses, and others, could be used to amplify the meaning of communal theological anthropology, the work of U.S. Latinax[15] theologians deserves particular notice. Popular religious practices have been common among many groups of Catholic faithful for many generations, yet it was U.S. Latinax theologians in the early 1980s who not only recognized these practices as a *locus theologicus* for constructive Catholic theology but saw in them the possibility of deeper appropriation of communal sensibilities.[16] Examples of such practices include dramatic reenactments: the passion of Jesus Christ; the narrative of Guadalupe's apparitions to Juan Diego; the Posadas, Mary and Joseph looking for lodging; and the Pastorela, a shepherds' play. And they include ritual practices: the leaving of small gifts for the Three Kings, *Los Reyes Magos*; the building of altars for All Saints' Day and All Souls' Day, *Día de los Muertos*; the creation of a prominent nativity scene during the extended Christmas season;[17] and the displaying of images of Guadalupe and various saints (*retablos*), in one's home and/or workspace.[18] In addition, these practices include the creation of installations and murals employing religious symbols in public spaces, for the purpose of protesting tragic murders, or the painful loss of a loved one.[19] As Latinax Catholic faithful participate in the various dimensions of these practices, they engage, wrestle with, and come to better understand the centrality of human interrelatedness. Human interrelatedness and interconnectivity are absorbed.

Early on, U.S. Latinax theologians recognized the formational dimension of these practices and affirmed that embedded within them was a sense that "community is understood to be fundamentally *preexistent* (therefore involuntary) and *constitutive*."[20] Such an understanding of human interrelatedness has a capacity to deepen awareness of God in our midst and to create communal spaces that turn persons' attention to the challenge of justice. And as I have argued elsewhere, the symbols embedded in communal practice can serve the purpose of ensuring a community's survival, materially and spiritually.[21]

In brief, a communal theological anthropology recognizes that the God-human relation is invariably mediated through human interrelatedness. Human interrelatedness entails our immanent relationships across the span of our lifetimes, and well beyond our lifetimes. Far more than our personal relationships, this includes our relationships with persons with whom we do not share a common language, a common nation-state, a common faith, a common historical or cultural worldview, or common life experience. And, when we recognize our relationship with those who are "other" than ourselves, then this recognition creates the space for heightened awareness of those who suffer, in particular, those who suffer as a result of injustice. Because they are most often based on biblical stories that turn our attention to those who suffer, Latinax popular religious practices encourage greater awareness of the suffering of others and animate a commitment to building a more just world.[22] Indeed a communal theological anthropology, as reflected in such practices, invites the creation of a new social consciousness, one more attuned to injustice and its resulting suffering, and a social consciousness that points toward solidarity.

Solidarity

Awareness of the suffering in the world encourages empathetic response to those suffering and the vulnerable. A communal theological anthropology becomes real and palpable when empathetic responses are indeed one-to-one responses yet are also more. Far too often, we regard the suffering of others in dichotomized ways that separate the analysis of an individual's experience of suffering from the social experience of suffering. For example, our dichotomized ways of thinking keep separate the racially motivated murder of one person *from* systemic racism or ill health *from* poverty, among many others. As I have previously written, "When these common and accepted dichotomies frame the discussion of suffering,...then we no longer can grasp with clarity either the way in which human suffering is at once both collective and individual or that the ways of 'experiencing pain and trauma can be both local and global.' We need an approach to suffering that subverts these typical dichotomies."[23] Elsewhere, I have argued for and named this approach *a social suffering hermeneutic*: "This self-conscious hermeneutic fosters an awareness of how conventional social experience can appear to be 'natural' and 'normal.' Yet this 'appearance' of normality, while ubiquitous, often conceals the workings of power that inflict suffering on the vulnerable and innocent among us."[24] Empathetic responses to those who suffer must stretch to embrace the praxis of solidarity, which is a pattern of acting motivated and informed by Jesus's vision of the coming Reign of God.

A communal theological anthropology of its very nature not only prompts questions about *who* is suffering and *why* they are suffering, but also directs attention to the significance of solidarity for all would-be disciples of Jesus Christ. Solidarity is intrinsically communal, as Pope Francis has made clear:

> Solidarity means much more than engaging in sporadic acts of generosity. It means thinking and acting in terms of community. It means that the lives of all are prior to the appropriation of goods by a few. It also means combatting the structural causes of poverty, inequality, the lack of work, land and housing, the denial of social and labor rights. It means confronting the destructive effects of the empire of money.[25]

As disciples of Jesus Christ, we must dare to stand at the foot of the cross of those who know crucifixion in our time, those whose lives are sacrificed on the altar of money, of sexual gratification, and of a myriad of other heinous evils of today, all of which victimize those loved by Jesus Christ. Solidarity requires a self-giving love poured out on behalf of sisters and brothers who have been despised, afflicted, impoverished, and victimized. Christ is to be found at the foot of the cross alongside these sisters and brothers.

Through the praxis of solidarity, the distinctiveness of the "other" remains wholly recognized, and those seeking to be in solidarity also retain their own distinctiveness, as M. Shawn Copeland has taught.[26] In this process, no one's humanity is reduced or caricatured. For solidarity to be authentic, the forged solidaristic relationships, whether they are newly formed or long-standing, are marked by a quality of mutuality such that the particularity and integrity of all parties are seen and recognized. Each comes to discover in the context of their relationships a new depth of understanding and appreciation of what it means to be human. No doubt, this new depth manifests itself as an offer of God's grace. Solidarity always involves recognizing the humanity of the "other" in all their otherness. Thus, solidarity requires of all parties an openness to the otherness of the "others." As Copeland says, "Openness implies receptivity, that is, a willingness to receive the other and to be received by the other in mutual relationship, to take on obligation with and to the other."[27]

A praxis of solidarity is orientated by the conviction that another world is possible, that together—with the despised, the poor, and the exploited of this world—we can build a society more in keeping with God's reign. That is, we can build a society committed to a more just, fair, and respectful treatment of all its members, in particular those who find themselves at the peripheries. Again Pope Francis reminds us, "We are called to reach out to those who find themselves in the existential peripheries of our societies and to show particular solidarity with the most vulnerable of our brothers and sisters: the poor, the disabled, the unborn and the sick, migrants and refugees, the elderly and the young who lack employment."[28] Such a commitment always means more than simply an expansion of the goods of society so that they now include the despised, the poor, and the oppressed. This alone is not sufficient. Solidarity entails an a priori commitment to those on the margins. In other words, the living conditions of those at the peripheries must function as *the norm* for judging our praxis of solidarity. God invites our conversion to the "other." Response means that we endeavor to see fully and to be so moved by the concrete particulars of the lives of those living along society's peripheries, that we place ourselves and all that we are at the disposal of a solidarity that strives to realize the common good. The praxis of solidarity is a path of ongoing conversion, a path that opens us to the possibility of grace.

Solidarity has as its goal the building up of the common good, that is, working to improve the conditions of society to the benefit of every human being so that each is able to pursue and realize the proper goals of life. By contrast, the common good must *not* be understood as a world in which the individualism of every human being is allowed to flourish. Pope Francis writes,

> Individualism does not make us more free, more equal, more fraternal. The mere sum of individual interest is not capable of generating a better world for the whole human family. Nor can it save us from the many ills that are now increasingly globalized. Radical individualism is a virus that is extremely difficult to eliminate, for it is clever. It makes us believe that everything consists in giving free rein to our own ambitions, as if by pursuing ever greater ambitions and creating safety nets we would somehow be serving the common good.[29]

Each human being around the world possesses an inalienable God-given dignity without any qualification. Accordingly, the rights that each of us have must be understood within the larger context of the common good. If we fail to recognize this greater good, our societies will devolve into a morass of conflicts and violence that over time will take us down the path of sociocide, the killing of society. Conversely, a commitment to the common good moves us in the direction of humanity's future.

> If every human being possesses an inalienable dignity, if all people are my brothers and sisters, and if the world truly belongs to everyone, then it matters little whether my neighbor was born in my country or elsewhere. My own country also shares responsibility for his or her development, although it can fulfil that responsibility in a variety of ways. It can offer a generous welcome to those in urgent need, or work to improve living conditions in their native lands by refusing to exploit those countries or to drain them of natural resources, backing corrupt systems that hinder the dignified development of their peoples.[30]

Formation for justice calls for courage and imagination on behalf of the common good, and it requires an openness to conversion.

Conversion—Moving the Human Heart

The praxis of solidarity necessitates conversion, ongoing conversion. Given that solidarity is "a moral virtue and social attitude born of personal conversion," as Pope Francis claims, then indeed solidarity "calls for commitment on the part of those responsible for education and formation."[31] Educators must consider what captivates the human heart such that an openness to conversion becomes a possibility, an ongoing conversion to the geographical and existential peripheries. Without attention to the *how* of conversion, theological education will encourage neither a praxis of solidarity nor the creation of a more just world.

While Christian theology has long rightly assumed the task of developing reasoned, intelligent, public arguments for the claims being advanced, reason alone has never been sufficient. Theologizing must encourage a longing and desire for God. A cogent argument, while crucial, will not sufficiently compel a transformation of human thinking, feeling, and ways of living. Transformation on all these levels requires a newfound appreciation, an experience that moves the human heart. Theology too often is taught in a manner that fails to support a way of life, such as a praxis of solidarity, because of its all-but-exclusive focus on conceptual content and its depreciation of the knowledge that is communicated through compelling symbols, dramatic speech, powerful narratives, and moving music, among other forms of art.

To a great degree, conversion comes about by attending to what moves the human heart. As theological educators, we will want to consider *how* theological education encourages students not only *to act* on behalf of a more just world and *to understand* clearly the nature of the Reign of God, but also how it emboldens students *to desire* ardently a more just world and a life of solidarity with those at the peripheries. In other words, how will theological education animate zeal for the Reign of God? Indeed, *orthopathy* is every bit as integral to a formative theological education as *orthopraxis* and *orthodoxy*. Orthopathy has to do with "the correct way of letting ourselves be affected by the reality of Christ,"[32] thus how our desires and affections are directed toward God's Reign.

While much has been written on the nature of conversion, our understanding of conversion limps along when it lacks an appreciation of that which affectively draws us to God. The experience of being drawn has to do with the capaciousness of our anagogical imagination, our awareness of God when we are moved by an experience of genuine beauty. "This movement of the heart is the 'spark,' the 'lighting of the fuse,' that inspires and sets in motion the interpretation of the Good and the True," as Alejandro García-Rivera has taught us.[33] An anagogical imagination is distinct from what David Tracy calls the Catholic analogical imagination.

U.S. Latinax theologians have long recognized the ways in which popular religious practices function as practices of beauty, animating and expanding our anagogical imaginations by heightening a consciousness of God. Affect plays a role here. In order to draw the human heart toward the good, and foster a human heart desirous of a more just world, cultivation of an anagogical imagination is needed. Simone Weil describes the *how* of this dimension of conversion when she writes, "The soul's natural inclination to love beauty is the trap God most frequently uses in order to win it and open it to the breath from on high."[34]

A communal theological anthropology is the cornerstone for the transforming work of justice. It makes teaching theology in the idiom of justice possible. Deepening familiarity with this rich anthropological starting block will enable students not only to *hear* Jesus's message of hope, but to *engage* in the ongoing work of liberation, and to *be and live* in the here and now of God's reign.

NOTES

1. Francis, Encyclical on Fraternity and Social Friendship *Fratelli tutti*, October 3, 2020, §171, https://www.vatican.va/content/francesco/en/encyclicals/documents/papa-francesco_20201003_enciclica-fratelli-tutti.html.

2. *Fratelli tutti*, §126.

3. *Fratelli tutti*, §127. The inner quotation is taken from Pope Francis's "Address on Nuclear Weapons" (Atomic Bomb Hypocenter Park, Nagasaki, Japan, November 24, 2019), *L'Osservatore Romano*, November 25–26, 2019, 6.

4. Paul Woodruff, *Reverence: Renewing a Forgotten Virtue* (New York: Oxford University Press, 2001), 4.

5. John Markey, "The Need for the Recovery of the Communal Dimension of Individual Spirituality" (unpublished paper).

6. Roberto S. Goizueta, *Caminemos con Jesús: Toward a Hispanic/Latino Theology of Accompaniment* (Maryknoll, NY: Orbis Books, 1995), 54.

7. Goizueta, *Caminemos con Jesús*, 59.

8. Goizueta, *Caminemos con Jesús*, 57.

9. Goizueta, *Caminemos con Jesús*, 64–65.

10. Catherine Mowry LaCugna, *God for Us: The Trinity and Christian Life* (San Francisco: Harper San Francisco, 1991); Elizabeth A. Johnson, *She Who Is: The Mystery of God in Feminist Theological Discourse* (New York: Crossroad, 1992).

11. M. Shawn Copeland, *Enfleshing Freedom: Body, Race, and Being* (Minneapolis, MN: Fortress Press, 2010), 55–105.

12. Kenneth R. Himes et al., eds., *Modern Catholic Social Teaching: Commentaries and Interpretations* (Washington, DC: Georgetown University Press, 2005).

13. Copeland, *Enfleshing Freedom*; Kelly Brown Douglas, *Stand Your Ground: Black Bodies and the Justice of God* (Maryknoll, NY: Orbis Books, 2015); Delores Williams, *Sisters in the Wilderness: The Challenge of Womanist God-Talk* (Maryknoll, NY: Orbis Books, 1993); Emilie M. Townes, *Womanist Ethics and the Cultural Production of Evil* (New York: Palgrave Macmillan, 2007).

14. Lisa Isherwood and Elaine Bellchambers, eds., *Through Us, With Us, In Us: Relational Theologies in the Twenty-First Century* (London: SCM Press, 2010).

15. In my work, I do not use *Hispanic* because this term has been used often in the United States to promote the assimilation of Latinax peoples into the Euro-American culture and/or to negate the value of the cultures from Latin American countries. In addition, *Hispanic* is a term often used to privilege Spanish roots and to minimize Indigenous roots. I use "Latinax" to refer to people of Latin American ancestry. The "a" in Latinax affirms the contributions made by Latina women

(often overlooked), and the "x" in Latinax recognizes both the fluidity of sexual orientation and identity, and the limitations to thinking strictly in male/female binary terms.

16. Alex García-Rivera, "The Whole and the Love of Difference: Latino Metaphysics as Cosmology," in *From the Heart of Our People: Latino/a Explorations in Catholic Systematic Theology*, ed. Miguel H. Díaz and Orlando O. Espín (Maryknoll, NY: Orbis Books, 1999), 54–83.

17. Timothy M. Matovina, "Hispanic Faith and Theology," *Journal of Family Ministry* 15, no. 3 (Fall 2001): 10–15.

18. Alex García-Rivera, *St. Martín de Porres: The Little Stories and the Semiotics of Culture* (Maryknoll, NY: Orbis Books, 1995); Ana María Pineda, "Imágenes de Dios en el Camino: Retablos, Ex-Votos, Milagritos, and Murals," *Theological Studies* 65 (2004): 364–79.

19. Nancy Pineda-Madrid, *Suffering and Salvation in Ciudad Juárez* (Minneapolis, MN: Fortress, 2011); Alyshia Gálvez, *Guadalupe in New York: Devotion and the Struggle for Citizenship Rights among Mexican Immigrants* (New York: New York University Press, 2010).

20. Goizueta, *Caminemos con Jesús*, 65.

21. Pineda-Madrid, *Suffering and Salvation*, 98.

22. See, for example, Pineda-Madrid, *Suffering and Salvation*; Gálvez, *Guadalupe in New York*.

23. Pineda-Madrid, *Suffering and Salvation*, 19.

24. Pineda-Madrid, *Suffering and Salvation*, 25.

25. *Fratelli tutti*, §116.

26. Copeland, *Enfleshing Freedom*, 89–90.

27. Copeland, *Enfleshing Freedom*, 94–95.

28. Francis, Message to Cardinal Kurt Koch on the Occasion of the 10th General Assembly of the World Council of Churches, October 4, 2013, https://www.vatican.va/content/francesco/en/messages/pont-messages/2013/documents/papa-francesco_20131004_world-council-churches.html. See also Francis, Apostolic Exhortation on the Proclamation of the Gospel in Today's World, *Evangelii gaudium*, November 24, 2013, §§19–49, 176–258, https://www.vatican.va/content/francesco/en/apost_exhortations/documents/papa-francesco_esortazione-ap_20131124_evangelii-gaudium.html.

29. *Fratelli tutti*, §105.

30. *Fratelli tutti*, §125.

31. *Fratelli tutti*, §114. See also Thomas C. Fox, "Francis Pre-Conclave Remarks Echo in First General Audience," *National Catholic Reporter*, March 27, 2013, https://www.ncronline.org/blogs/ncr-today/francis-pre-conclave-remarks-echo-first-general-audience.

32. Jon Sobrino, *Christ the Liberator: A View from the Victims* (Maryknoll, NY: Orbis Books, 2001), 210.

33. Alejandro García-Rivera, *The Community of the Beautiful: A Theological Aesthetics* (Collegeville, MN: Liturgical Press, 1999), 185. See also my "¡Somos Criaturas de Dios!—Seeing and Beholding the Garden of God," in *Planetary Solidarity: Global Women's Voices on Christian Doctrine and Climate Justice*, ed. Grace Ji-Sun Kim and Hilda P. Koster (Minneapolis, MN: Fortress Press, 2017): 311–24.

34. Simone Weil, "Forms of the Implicit Love of God," in *Waiting for God* (New York: G. P. Putman's Sons, 1951), 163.

Part Three

HOPES AND OUTCOMES

7

FOSTERING COMMUNITIES THAT PRAY AND CELEBRATE

John F. Baldovin, SJ

THE CATHOLIC LITURGY as it has been reformed in the wake of Vatican II is one of the more sensitive issues in theological education and formation. At the same time, the formation of a sacramental imagination is vital to the Catholic tradition and more and more relevant to the life of other Christian communities as well. This essay will focus both on the experience of liturgy within a school setting and on the academic aspects of liturgical formation. A third section will focus on formation for liturgical practice specifically in Catholic ministerial schools.

Experience

After nearly four decades of teaching liturgy in theological-ministerial programs, I have come to the conclusion that experience usually wins out over classroom instruction when it comes to how liturgy exercises a formative influence. In addition to and often despite what they learn in the classroom, the cumulative effect of experience forms our students. As Gilles Routhier has put it well, "Liturgical formation from the perspective of practical theology is somehow a liturgical formation by the liturgy itself."[1]

Much of what students have experienced before their formal education in liturgy and/or sacraments will differ significantly from what they experience at school. Sad to say, often enough that experience has been lacking quality and vitality. Or what they experience in a school setting may lack the cultural dynamics that they may have experienced in their own contexts. On the other hand, a (growing?) minority of students come from a traditionalist Catholic liturgical experience that rejects what schools have to offer.

My experience in both undergraduate teaching and ministerial formation has led me to the conviction that liturgies in the school setting need to be very carefully prepared. They also need to offer some variety. In many schools, several Sunday liturgies are offered that cater to different backgrounds and interests, for example, more traditional music (in the morning) and more contemporary music (in the evening). Music is where most creativity will be found since the Catholic liturgy is somewhat constrained by what I will call a "code." More on this below. In the setting of a ministerial school, it is probably most useful to blend styles of music as well as the use of languages that reflect the student body.

Another issue to be considered in liturgical formation in the school setting is preparation for what students will experience after they have finished their degrees. A school liturgy may be of great quality, but if it differs too much from what students will experience later on, it will not have ongoing formative value. Here, I think that consistency in the quality of music, preaching, and the formation of a community that prays together will be a good omen.

Of course, liturgy is not limited to the Eucharist. Other forms of liturgy like adoration of the Blessed Sacrament, which is increasingly popular among younger students, can be rather creative within the Roman Catholic context and give more opportunity for lay leadership, as can the celebration of the church's common prayer, the Liturgy of the Hours. Various forms of services like ecumenical and/or interfaith prayer will also provide opportunities for creativity and lay leadership. The recent coronavirus pandemic has inspired a great deal of creativity (most of it lay-driven) with online liturgical experiences.

We also need to recognize that all liturgy encourages us to put our bodies where our mouths are. I am very fond of the story that has been attributed variously to Isadora Duncan or to Martha Graham, both pioneers of modern dance. After a premiere, a reporter asked the choreographer what the dance meant. The answer: "Darling, if I could have told you what it meant, we wouldn't have had to dance it." Voilà, the embodied nature of Christian worship in a nutshell. Liturgical experience thus promotes the integration of the analytic aspects of theological education with the richness of symbol and ritual. In liturgy the nonverbal communicates as much as the verbal does.

Needless to say, all this means that great care and a good deal of work and *patience* needs to go into the preparation of liturgical experience. Liturgical formation is rarely if ever an earthshaking, one-off event. Liturgical formation, as much as any aspect of formation, is cumulative.

In addition to embodiment and the appreciation of ritual and symbol, there are other important formative factors in liturgical experience. For Catholics, when the liturgy is celebrated with care and fidelity, the experience will ideally foster a renewed sense of the common priesthood of the baptized that is so central to the post–Vatican II reformed liturgy. Liturgy is a team sport, a cooperative venture, and good liturgical experience emphasizes how we are all in this together. That is why the Council's Constitution on the Sacred Liturgy (*Sacrosanctum concilium*) insists on the "full, conscious, and active participation" of the faithful in all liturgical services.[2] Here we find a theology of the church in action as the Episcopal theologian and liturgical scholar, Louis Weil, has pointed out many times.[3]

Once again, ideally, consistently good liturgical celebration is formative of character, attitudes, and virtues. The moral and ethical ideals of the scriptures are reinforced in our liturgical prayers and actions and in turn form them. This is why Vatican II insisted that that liturgy is both the summit and the source of the Christian life.

We cannot neglect a major challenge that, in today's digital and virtual world, has only been exacerbated. Not only for Catholics but for many Christians, liturgy has traditionally been a primarily devotional and not a communal activity. This should come as no surprise in a society so obsessed with individualism and addicted to consumerism. It is very difficult to appreciate that liturgy has a certain prior claim on us because it is God's gift before it is our own response. One of the greatest challenges facing those responsible for liturgical formation is to foster a worship atmosphere where community can truly thrive.

Theory

Let's turn then to the more academic side of liturgical formation. After all, in the school setting liturgical formation is not only *through* the liturgy but also *for* the liturgy.[4] Although I have acknowledged the priority of the experiential aspect of liturgical formation, academic instruction is formative as well. On the undergraduate level, courses in liturgy and sacraments will most likely be elective, but even there great good can be done in informing students of the richness of the Christian worship tradition as well as forming them for sensitivity to the ritual and symbolic dimensions of all worship.

Regarding schools that prepare candidates for ministry, the Liturgy Constitution of Vatican II marked a radical shift by mandating courses on the liturgy.[5] Prior to Vatican II, liturgy had mainly been a subfield of canon law. Practical instruction aimed primarily at preventing mistakes in the rubrics (often considered sinful!) instead of a style of celebration, now commonly referred to as the *Ars Celebrandi*.

Now many Catholic ministerial schools educate both ordained and lay candidates and so will have a variety of programs aimed at different outcomes. Priesthood candidates are normally required to take at least an introduction to liturgy, a rites practicum, a homiletics (preaching) course, and a confessions (penance) practicum. All of these courses are open to lay candidates of course. A preaching course will be very useful for lay ecclesial ministers. A course specifically focused on lay presiding is also desirable.

What can be hoped for in terms of specifically academic formation? At the very least I would hope that students learn how to situate the study of liturgy within the broader project of theology and with other ministerial goals, such as pastoral care and the life of a Christian community. Students also need to appreciate liturgical theology (including consideration of symbol, myth, and language) and history as well as important elements that affect worship, like music and the built environment. In an increasingly multicultural society, students need to value and appreciate the various cultural contributions of the groups that make up modern American Catholicism.

In this vein I offer students a scheme that I entitle: *Core, Code, Culture/Context*. For Catholics, liturgy and sacraments include an essential *core* including proclamation of the Word, the sacred meal

(Eucharist) and the bath in water (baptism). But this core never exists in the abstract. It is *encoded* in a Catholic way of doing things like a specific liturgical cycle of feasts and seasons and a basic, commonly celebrated ritual procedure. One can think here of the various Marian feasts of the liturgical year and the basic structure of the lectionary. But core and code are ultimately insufficient. The liturgy is never abstract. Like a drama that exists in written form, liturgy must be enacted. And it is always enacted in a specific time and place by this particular community with its history and cultural heritage. Thus, there is no such thing as "liturgy in general." This is why students need to be helped to understand how and why liturgy has changed and will continue to change *culturally and contextually* even while respecting the core and the code. No doubt all of this is a daunting task in the classroom and one can hope that other academic courses will enable students to see important connections between liturgy and the other areas of theology and ministerial formation.

In addition, although students' prior experience is a boon, it can also constitute a challenge. Often enough students will come to the study of liturgy with strongly held opinions and feelings, even though these may be based on a rather minimal knowledge base. In other words, they are sometimes eager to criticize the liturgy (which is certainly not beyond criticism) before they adequately understand it. Therefore, I find it a challenge to help students to distinguish what they know from what they think and from what they feel. Like any ritual and symbolic activity, liturgy often stirs deep feelings, so respecting the balance between knowing, thinking, and feeling can be daunting.

A further challenge is constituted by the very fact that a good education in liturgy inspires students to become critical of liturgical practice. I cannot count the number of times over the years that students have told me (half-jokingly) that I have "ruined them for Christian worship." Having a critical eye is an understandable result of a deepened knowledge of the liturgy. Therefore, it is also incumbent upon the instructor to encourage a kind of second naïveté when it comes to practice. In other words, once one has done the critical work of study as in historical-critical exegesis of the Bible, one might approach the liturgy with a certain amount of skepticism. Clearly to stop there would be disastrous for a life of worship. Therefore, it is necessary to come back to the theological and spiritual conviction that the liturgy is primarily God's work before it is our own. Even when our own efforts leave something to be desired, Catholics believe that God is at work. This is basically what we mean by the Latin phrase *ex opere operato*. Catholics believe that God is infallibly at work when the liturgy is celebrated properly. This is not to say that mere adherence to rules and rubrics is desirable, but the very fact of the liturgy celebrated correctly means that God's self-gift (grace) is on offer. At the same time we should hope that students will not settle for the minimal.

How might the study of liturgy fit into the theological-ministerial curriculum as a whole? Many people are familiar with the traditional Latin tag, *lex orandi, lex credendi*, that is, the rule of praying and the rule of believing are intimately related.[6] One can argue that often enough liturgy precedes the formulation of faith. Hence the importance of liturgical study for the entire curriculum. Liturgy, after all, is where the scriptures come alive for most Christians. As many have argued, the Bible is a book that is born of the Christian assembly.[7] Mind you this takes some explanation today when access to printed or electronic versions of the Bible are so readily available and most people presuppose that true appreciation of the Bible begins in the classroom or the library rather than in the practice of worship.

In addition, the contemporary Roman Rite allows for a great deal of freedom in the choice of texts to be sung as part of the liturgy. In fact, music is integral to liturgical *celebration*, as all but the aesthetically insensitive can recognize. The music itself has a powerful formative influence on the Christian affections. The lyrics (for good or for ill, since not all texts are equal) can have a lasting effect on how people digest and express what they believe. Think of how a particular piece of liturgical music may "stay in your head" or listen to children as they repeatedly sing what they have heard in church.

Further, the study of liturgy ideally influences how ministerial students integrate their understanding of virtues, the moral life, and social justice. Frequently, people think that work for justice and liturgical celebration are discrete—or even opposing—facets of Christian life. Good instruction in the liturgy should open up the profound moral and justice dimensions that are embedded in the liturgy itself. For example, reconciliation, communion, the exchange of peace, and intercessions are all elements that open up the justice dimension of the liturgy.[8]

These considerations on the academic side of liturgical formation for ministry can be appreciated via another traditional term, *mystagogy*.

In the early church, mystagogy (roughly, an explanation of the Christian mysteries or sacraments) was a kind of adult pedagogy by which the newly baptized, confirmed, and communicated were instructed about what had happened to them in their initiation on the basis of their experience. Often, they were not given the "game plan" of the liturgy beforehand but rather allowed to experience the rites first.[9] Academic instruction in liturgy can be mystagogical in that it capitalizes on experience in order to deepen one's understanding of the liturgy.

Finally, to repeat a theme introduced above under experience, academic liturgical instruction should enable students to appreciate all the more the embodied nature of liturgical celebration, since the liturgy is one very important space for lived Christian experience. Needless to say, students need to appreciate this embodiment not only for themselves but should learn how to communicate it to others.

Teaching Practice

Since liturgical formation is not only *by* the liturgy but *for* the liturgy, the practical dimension of liturgical leadership and other forms of ministry is an essential element in the preparation of most if not all ministerial students. Since in the Roman Catholic Church there are candidates for lay ecclesial ministry as well as candidates for ordained ministry, there will naturally be some distinction in the practical courses given. However desirable some may find a broadening of the pool of candidates for ordination, the current situation requires a division of courses for lay and ordination candidates.

Especially in view of the many current opportunities for preaching in cyberspace, it makes a good deal of sense for all ministerial candidates to take homiletics courses together. I think of the weekly online homilies given by "Women Preach," sponsored by Future Church.[10] Even though giving a homily (technically speaking) at a Eucharist is reserved to priests and deacons, this form of preaching is far from the only kind of preaching possible. In terms of formation, it seems to me that all students can benefit from a diversity of backgrounds, genders, cultures, and points of view in their homiletic preparation—just as they do in their academic classes. Preaching is itself extremely formative in that will encourage students to further digest and synthesize what they learn in their academic courses like scripture and systematic theology.

While not exactly forming students in the same ways as catechesis or religious education, honing abilities for preaching promotes similar skills in communicating the gospel. What is it about Christian faith that students have so thoroughly digested that they can speak out of a well-synthesized or holistic vision of Christianity? Lastly, they need to be in solidarity with their listeners and realize that they are speaking to themselves as much as they are to others. We're all challenged to put what we talk about into practice.

I turn finally to formation for liturgical presiding. Here there will certainly be a division of tasks since the liturgy requires different roles and there are restrictions about who can exercise them. (Although the diaconate for women is an open question.) There are, however, a number of presidential roles that are open to lay ministers: communion outside of Mass, communion of the sick, ministry to the dying, and leadership of the Liturgy of the Hours.[11] Lay ecclesial ministers will also frequently be tasked with helping to prepare various liturgies in their pastoral settings.

On the other hand, all of our students, lay-ministerial and ordination candidates alike, face one common challenge. To preside is to communicate with one's body. The academic context does not normally reward the graceful use of the body, but the body is essential to effective presiding. Remember the story attributed to Isadora Duncan or Martha Graham mentioned above. Body language will reveal whether or not a presider is comfortable in the role.[12] This is of course where the healthy human-formation dimension of theological formation is essential. Without it, presiders will not be able to perform their primary task, which is to pray in public so as to help others to pray together as the Body of Christ. As Louis Weil wisely observes in "The Shape of Liturgical Formation," students need to be helped to appreciate that the liturgy combines both "Godward" and "People-ward" elements.[13] To ignore one in favor of the other is to do our worship an injustice.

At the same time students can be taught various skills in presiding such as how to walk, how to use gesture, how to speak, where to look, and even how to sit. Sometimes, especially among the very intellectually capable, students need to be convinced of the importance of these skills. Our excellent academic training can *sometimes* lead us to think that only the rational aspects of what the liturgy communicates really count. I think of the marvelous words of Robert Hovda in an essay on liturgical vestments:

> Like so many sense experiences that rationalist types dismiss as trivial, liturgical vesture has a considerable impact on the feelings of the assembly as a whole as well as on those exercising a particular role of leadership. Anyone who contrary to the most elementary human experience, persists in the stubborn conviction that ideas, points, arguments are the stuff that move human beings, is natively unfit for liturgical leadership, if not for liturgical life.[14]

A sine qua non for liturgical presiding in the contemporary Roman Catholic Church is the ability to coordinate with other ministers. The post–Vatican II Catholic liturgy is not a solo performance but rather, as I noted above, a cooperative venture. The liturgy, and especially but not only the celebration of the Eucharist, requires a number of ministers: readers, deacons, servers, musicians, and others. To imagine that these are mere window dressing is to miss the point of the liturgical reform of the past sixty years—the ministers represent the assembly in its fullness as the embodiment here and now of Christ's baptismal priesthood.

Conclusion

This essay has highlighted the many challenges and opportunities involved in the celebration of liturgy as well as the teaching of liturgy as formative. I am more convinced than ever that helping our students to appreciate and gain fruit from the specifically communal dimension of liturgy as well as the vital connection between our worship and the rest of our lives is essential to holistic formation. As I have noted above, the obstacles are formidable, but if we Catholics really believe that God is truly at work in calling us to worship and being present with us in it, it is all well worth the effort. This is what we can call the sacramental imagination. The liturgy helps us to see all created reality in a sacramental light, that is, illuminated by and filled with God's presence. By the same token, seeing God at work in creation comes to fruition in our liturgies. Helping students to understand this important reality is vital to their development as Christians. It is also crucial for ministers who will impart this vision to others.

At the 2019 Assembly of the Vatican Congregation for Worship and the Discipline of the Sacraments, Pope Francis emphasized the importance of liturgical formation, giving a certain priority to practice over ideas.[15] This is a frequent theme in Francis's pontificate—the need to attend to reality before we impose our ideas upon it. One very important aspect of the Christian reality is manifested when Christians join in common worship. This is one of the places where "the rubber meets the road." Since all of the baptized are in this together, it is incumbent on all theological educators as well as ministerial formators, not only those who specialize in liturgy, to be attentive to the liturgical formation of our students—in both theory and practice.

NOTES

1. Gilles Routhier, "Liturgical Formation," *Studia Liturgica* 46 (2016): 53. The entirety of this issue of *Studia Liturgica* consists of papers from the 25th Congress of the international ecumenical Societas Liturgica. The theme of the congress was liturgical formation.

2. Vatican Council II, Constitution on the Sacred Liturgy, *Sacrosanctum concilium*, December 4, 1963, 14, https://www.vatican.va/archive/hist_councils/ii_vatican_council/documents/vat-ii_const_19631204_sacrosanctum-concilium_en.html.

3. For example, in Weil's "The Shape of Liturgical Formation: Vertical/Horizontal, Horizontal/Vertical," *Sewanee Theological Review* 52 (2008): 33–47.

4. See Thomas Whelan, "The 'Reign of God' as Primary Goal of Liturgical Formation," *Studia Liturgica* 47 (2017): 61–73.

5. See *Sacrosanctum concilium*, §16.

6. For a recent treatment of this adage as well as a valuable work on liturgy as a field of study, see Joris Geldhof, *Liturgical Theology as a Research Program* (Leiden: Brill, 2020). For *lex orandi, lex credendi*, see Geldhof, 2–6.

7. See, for example, Gordon Lathrop, *The Four Gospels on Sunday: The New Testament and the Reform of Christian Worship* (Minneapolis: Fortress Press, 2012).

8. See the wonderful essay by Robert Hovda, "The Amen Corner: Where Have You Been? Peace Liturgies Are the Only Kind We Have," *Worship* 57 (1983): 438–43.

9. See Edward Yarnold, *The Awe-Inspiring Rites of Initiation: The Origins of the RCIA*, 2nd ed. (Collegeville, MN: Liturgical Press, 1994). For an excellent example, see Goffredo Boselli, *The Spiritual Meaning of the Liturgy: School of Prayer, Source of Life*, trans. Barry Hudock (Collegeville, MN: Liturgical Press, 2014).

10. See the Catholic Women Preach website at https://www.catholicwomenpreach.org/.

11. See National Conference of Catholic Bishops, *A Ritual for Lay Persons: Rites for Holy Communion and the Pastoral Care of the Sick and Dying* (Collegeville, MN: Liturgical Press, 1993).

12. See Eileen Maggiore, "Catechesis and Faith Formation: Classroom Teaching Practices as Embodied, Contextual Liturgical Formation," *New Theology Review* 30, no. 2 (2018): 55–58.

13. Weil, "Shape of Liturgical Formation," 33.

14. Robert Hovda, "The Vesting Liturgical Ministers," *Worship* 54 (1980): 103.

15. See Francis, "Address to Participants at the Plenary Assembly of the Congregation for Divine Worship and the Discipline of the Sacraments," February 14, 2019, https://www.vatican.va/content/francesco/en/speeches/2019/february/documents/papa-francesco_20190214_cong-culto-divino.html.

8

THEOLOGICAL EDUCATION THAT PROMOTES RESILIENCE

Melissa M. Kelley

IN EARLY 2020, life changed for vast swaths of the world as the coronavirus pandemic took hold, affecting virtually all aspects of experience. We are well familiar with the grim realities and costs of this scourge, and we continue to struggle with them. Early in 2023, close to seven million people around the world had died due to COVID-19. Almost three hundred million people have suffered from the virus, many with long-term negative effects.[1] In the United States, millions have endured unemployment, unstable housing, or food insecurity.[2] Countless workplaces, schools, and churches have closed for stretches of time, leaving families in the lurch and forcing faith communities to gather online, if at all. Rates of mental health crises have skyrocketed.[3] Global rates of domestic violence have also risen, as families have contended with terrible stress and as victims may have been unable to escape dangerous home situations due to mandatory lockdowns or restricted movement.[4] Gravely ill people have suffered and died alone in hospitals due to virus containment measures, and survivors have been unable to gather at religious services to pray and to accompany their loved ones on their final journeys.[5]

In the United States, the ongoing pandemic has exposed and exacerbated terrible polarizations in communities and families, as public health mandates and basic safety measures have become vigorously charged with political and religious meaning. Deep wounds and divides have been exposed concerning this country's entrenched racism, as millions have condemned the brutal killings of George Floyd and many other people of color at the hands of police, while others have denounced the activism of groups such as Black Lives Matter. Following the highly contentious presidential election in 2020, we watched ongoing efforts to delegitimate the certified results, as well as a deadly riot at the U.S. Capitol. Meanwhile, the effects of climate change are increasingly dire as wildfires and deadly storms wreak havoc. We also continue to witness the relentless suffering of countless refugees, war victims, and impoverished people around the world.

We live in such difficult times and must contend with chronic and even overwhelming stress and challenges. How do we keep going in ways that are healthful and hopeful? Further, how do we in theological education help ourselves and our students to engage and respond to terrible realities, both personally and professionally? It is hard to imagine responses to these questions that do not include a firm focus on *resilience*. We must be *resilient* if we are to move through fraught times without succumbing to stress, anxiety, exhaustion, and hopelessness. In this chapter, I consider the critical topic of *resilience* through the lenses of neuroscience, social science, and pastoral theology. I also posit that theological educators must embrace an intentional focus on resilience as an essential formative dimension of their teaching and mentoring. I trace specific elements of formative theological education that I think contribute powerfully to the development of resilience in students, and I suggest why the development of resilience in students and in ourselves is an essential project that connects to the heart of Christian faith and life.

Resilience and Neuroscience

If we have more than muddled through the great stressors of recent months and years, we have likely drawn considerably on our resilience. We may understand resilience as "a measure of the ability of an organism to adapt, and to withstand challenges to its stability."[6] For humans, the challenges to our stability that we must withstand include various types of stressors, that is, sources of strain or "threats to homeostasis."[7]

Beyond the coronavirus pandemic and the other struggles described above, the daily stressors that we may confront in our personal, familial, and communal lives are many. Even infants and young children may experience difficult stressors, such as neglect, illness, painful family dynamics, or learning challenges. Stress that is overwhelming or chronic can compromise our capacity to cope, leaving us unable to manage and perhaps struggling with hope. Resilience is an essential capacity for sustaining people at difficult or stressful moments and allowing for healing and hopeful living over time.

Because we live in the "emerging age of neuroscience,"[8] our understandings of the process and potential of resilience in the face of threats to stability have been augmented by important studies of the human brain over the lifespan. Such research strongly suggests that "the brain is the key organ that mobilizes the body's defenses, for better or worse, to remove the threats, and return the organism to homeostatic balance."[9] When difficult stressors occur during significant developmental periods, their negative effects upon resilience may be long-lasting. As Karatsoreos and McEwen note, "adverse childhood experiences can alter resilience of individuals, making it more difficult for them to respond normally to adverse situations in adulthood."[10] However, neuroscientific research also highlights the human potential for resilience, due to the wonders of neuroplasticity, that is, the capacity of the brain to continue to grow and change throughout the lifespan. Kirk Bingaman writes,

> Far from being fixed and unchanging, the human brain has a profound capacity for change, continued growth, and transformation of its own functioning *and* structure. And, this is not simply limited to the formative years of childhood and adolescence and even early adulthood for that matter, as certain developmental theories have suggested. Rather, the potential for neuroplasticity that is abundantly evident at the beginning of life extends across the human life cycle, and therefore is also available until the end of life.[11]

Through neuroplasticity, the human brain may change at any point in life, at least modestly so. Thus, those who have endured adverse childhood events may experience some mitigation of related negative effects.[12] Neuroscience makes clear that growth in resilience is always a possibility for human beings, and this reality is a source of profound hope as we contend with a global pandemic and other large-scale stressors while also managing more personal troubles.

Dimensions of Resilience: A Social-Science Perspective

How do we engage our brain's natural potential for growth in resilience, made possible through neuroplasticity? While research in multiple fields suggests various roads to resilience, some concrete correlates of resilience have been proposed by renowned psychiatrists and resilience researchers Steven Southwick and Dennis Charney.[13] Over many years, they have engaged and interviewed "a large number of highly resilient individuals"[14] who have adapted well following traumatic life events, such as violent assault or incarceration as prisoners of war, and they have identified ten dimensions or factors described most often by these survivors "as crucial, and sometimes even life-saving"[15] for their adaptation. Two of these factors are highly relevant to our consideration of formative theological education; they are *meaning/purpose* and *social support*.[16]

Southwick and Charney note that among their interview participants who are highly resilient, "most were active problem solvers who looked for meaning and opportunity in the midst of adversity and sometimes even found humor in the darkness."[17] Their search for and embrace of larger meaning fueled their will to survive and to adapt well following traumatic experiences. Their participants also frequently described how social networks and social support were essential to their survival and well-being: "Strong Ties Save Lives."[18] Thus, in considering the necessity of strengthening resilience for all of us living in taxing times, we must highlight the importance of meaning and social support for our well-being. These areas are also critical foci for work in formative theological education. As we focus intentionally on meaning and social support in our formative work with students, we may contribute powerfully to their hope-enhancing growth in resilience.

Pastoral-Theological Reflection on Resilience

While neuroscience and social scientific research offer illuminating understandings of resilience, I find it compelling to reflect on resilience through an explicitly Christian pastoral-theological lens, the heart of my own educational focus. From this perspective, I suggest that the essential road to resilience for the Christian runs directly through Christian faith and life. Core Christian theological meanings, commitments, and practices are incomparable sources of strength for our coping and of hope for our future. For illustrative purposes, some of these core elements will be considered briefly in light of the two resilience factors—meaning and social support—highlighted by Southwick and Charney.[19] However, these elements are much more than research findings; they are riches of Christian faith and life and foundational sources of our hopeful resilience.

MEANING AND NARRATIVE

As noted above, efforts to cope with great difficulty are substantially aided by a deep and abiding sense of meaning and purpose. As Nietzsche opined, "If you have your *why* for life, you can get by with almost any *how*."[20] Our ways of making meaning help to construct a sense of order and coherence in our lives; however, sometimes our meaning is shaken or even shattered by unexpected or difficult life events. We may fruitfully consider such an experience through a narrative lens. As constructivist psychologist Robert Neimeyer suggests, loss or stress may usher in deeply painful experiences of "narrative disruptions,"[21] that is, breaks in or interruptions to the life story we have planned or imagined for ourselves. With narrative disruption may come disrupted meaning, as our life story may no longer seem sensible or coherent and our ways of making meaning no longer plausible or valid. These disruptions may also lead us to question whether the future life story we have imagined remains a possibility. In such moments, we may struggle with the awful challenge of meaninglessness and despair. Given the important positive correlation of meaning and resilience, we can appreciate that disruptions to our life stories and our ways of making meaning may mightily undermine our resilience and capacity to hope.

An incredible gift of Christianity is the incomparable riches it provides for a life of meaning that holds and sustains us, even through the great struggles and suffering we will certainly know. For the Christian, narrative disruption, no matter how painful, ought not to generate loss of hopeful meaning. Our story is not ours alone, nor is it defined solely by the contours of our experiences. Rather, our story is embedded within and fully dependent upon the ultimately hopeful Story of God's saving action through the paschal mystery, "Christ's work of redemption accomplished principally by his Passion, death, Resurrection, and glorious Ascension, whereby 'dying he destroyed our death, rising he restored our life.'"[22] We may draw on deeply hopeful meaning even as we suffer and struggle because our finite story—however disrupted—is enveloped and defined by the paschal mystery, the Christ-events that have transformed all of history, that transcend human time, and that point always to life.

As the *Catechism of the Catholic Church* conveys:

> When his Hour comes, [Jesus] lives out the unique event of history which does not pass away: Jesus dies, is buried, rises from the dead, and is seated at the right hand of the Father "once for all." His Paschal mystery is a real event that occurred in our history, but it is unique: all other historical events happen once, and then they pass away, swallowed up in the past. The Paschal mystery of Christ, by contrast, cannot remain only in the past, because by his death he destroyed death, and all that Christ is—all that he did and suffered for all men—participates in the divine eternity, and so transcends all times while being made present in them all. The event of the Cross and Resurrection *abides* and draws everything toward life.[23]

Every human life includes stress, suffering, and narrative disruption. Yet we trust in the continuing work of Christ through the power of the Spirit, making whole what has been broken, renewing what has been dashed, and restoring coherence to disrupted life stories and shaken meaning. There is no disrupted narrative that cannot be rewritten in light of the saving events of the paschal mystery. There is no shaken meaning that cannot be restored by trust in God's love in Christ: "For God so loved the world that he gave his only Son, so that everyone who believes in him may not perish but may have eternal life" (John 3:16). For Christians, the deepest possible root of resilience is our trust that no matter what occurs in life, we cannot be separated from the love of God as revealed in the Christ events. "For I am convinced that neither death, nor life, nor angels, nor rulers, nor things present, nor things to come, nor powers, nor height, nor depth, nor anything else in all creation, will be able to separate us from the love of God in Christ Jesus our Lord" (Rom 8:38–39). This is our ultimate meaning and source of hope and life.

SOCIAL SUPPORT

Clearly, our understanding of the relationship of meaning and resilience is deeply enhanced through the lens of Christian faith. Likewise, we may come to see the interconnection of social support and resilience much more fully through this lens. Southwick and Charney[24] describe the strong correlation of social support and resilience; their highly resilient interview participants described the significance of social support as they adapted to traumatic life events. Deep and caring connections with others help us all to cope with and adapt well to the inevitable struggles in life. From a Christian perspective, the importance of social support is much more than a compelling research result; it is a central faith mandate: "I give you a new commandment, that you love one another. Just as I have loved you, you also should love one another" (John 13:34). The Christian community bears an essential responsibility to embody and enact care for one another and for the world; in so doing, we participate with God in God's love for humanity and all of creation. We must extend this care in a particular way to those who suffer due to injustice, lack of access to resources, or other aspects of oppression or marginalization. This includes those who do not have ready access to potential sources of resilience. Growing in resilience must never be a matter of privilege; all must have opportunity to thrive and live lives grounded in hope.

The Christian community also enacts essential social support through its witness to hope and trust in God's Story as revealed in Christ. When we participate together in the liturgical and sacramental life of the church, we dramatically affirm our communal story as the people of God. Through our shared prayerful words and ritual actions, our individual stories become increasingly enmeshed in and enveloped by the larger Story of hope that is God's Story. This Story provides ultimate support and sustenance through all the troubles that we might face in our lives, and we come to know, trust, and participate in this Story most fully through the community of faith. We need one another to engage in and attest to our shared faith Story, so that we may each recall and draw hope and sustenance from this Story when our own stories and meanings are disrupted. These vital, faith-based expressions of social support connect us to our deepest possible root of hopeful meaning and thus are essential sources of hopeful resilience.

Formative Theological Education and Resilience

Having considered select contemporary understandings of resilience as well as pastoral-theological reflection on some of its core aspects, we turn now to the area of formative theological education. The significant two-part question taken up here is this: For those of us who teach and mentor in seminaries and schools of theology and ministry, *why* is formation in resilience a critically important focus of our work, and *how* might we take up this focus on resilience with consistent intentionality? Graduate school can be a stressful experience, and graduate work in theology and ministry may be particularly challenging, as students develop their understandings of God, humanity, faith, life, and vocation. Graduate students often must balance studies with family, work, ministry, and community responsibilities. Beyond these expected stressors, our students have certainly contended with many of the losses and challenges associated with the coronavirus pandemic and other current crises described at the beginning of this chapter. A resilient life stance is a necessity for our students, perhaps now more than ever, as they likely confront narrative disruptions and shaken meanings. They will also need to be highly resilient after graduation; their work and ministry will be challenging and perhaps overwhelming as they teach, engage with, and support those enduring loss, crisis, or trauma. Significant research highlights the large risks for those in ministry of being emotionally overtaxed, enduring high levels of work stress, or facing occupational burnout.[25] These are not minor concerns.

Over time, ministers and others in helping professions who experience ongoing work stress may suffer terrible consequences. Christina Maslach writes,

> The person who burns out is unable to deal successfully with the chronic emotional stress of the job, and this failure to cope can be manifested in a number of ways, including low morale, impaired performance, absenteeism and high turnover. A common response to burnout is to "get out," by changing jobs, moving into administrative work, or even leaving the profession entirely.[26]

No one in theological education wants their graduates to burn out, leave their professions, and suffer ongoing distress. Therefore, we must understand our teaching and mentoring as providing a vital opportunity to foster resilience in our students so that they might cope well and avoid significant distress and even burnout when the stressors and disruptions of life occur. To consider more concretely this necessary commitment to fostering resilience in formative theological education, we might explicitly highlight again the areas of meaning and social support.

Boston College education professor and researcher Dennis Shirley emphasizes the necessity for educators to help students foster deep and rich meaning and purpose for their lives.[27] Above we have considered that the ultimate source of meaning for the Christian derives from trust that our story is embedded within and fully dependent upon the ultimately hopeful Story of God's saving action through the paschal mystery. From this perspective, an essential aspect of formative theological education that contributes to resilience would be intentional communication—both within the classroom and beyond—regarding this faith meaning so that students may grow in trust that their story rests within God's Story as revealed in Christ, thus grounding their capacity for resilience in the ultimate source of meaning. This communication should occur through direct classroom teaching, such as in a systematic theology course on hope or in a practical theology course on trauma and healing. This emphasis could also be part of additional formative elements, including preaching at liturgical gatherings and sharing at communal celebrations. In taking up this work, we must not reduce or oversimplify the full and complex material to be included in any graduate theological program, including substantial and nuanced treatments of suffering and mystery. Nevertheless, with a consistent focus on cultivating resilience in all areas of formative theological education, we must encourage and support hope and trust that our story rests within God's Story, and therefore our lives are grounded always in hopeful meaning, whatever challenges and disruptions we may endure.

Formative theological education committed to bolstering this hopeful meaning will also foster growth in the community, the Body of Christ. As described above, commitments and actions of the Christian community are an incomparable source of social support, a hallmark of resilience. This support is embodied as we care for one another and for the world; it is also enacted as we witness together to our shared faith Story, our essential source of hope and sustenance when our own stories and meanings are disrupted. In these concrete ways, we participate with God in God's ongoing creative work in the world. From this perspective, a critical part of our formative work in theological education is to cultivate community among students, faculty, and staff, as well as wider bodies such as neighborhoods, volunteer sites, and internship placements, as a means of encouraging such participation. In and through various expressions of community, we continue to learn together what it means to be the Body of Christ, caring for and sustaining one another through personal and communal struggles and challenges. For example, students, faculty, and staff may gather regularly for liturgical worship, an opportunity to cultivate resilience in multiple ways. All gathered have the priceless opportunity to reflect on their own lives and contemporary dimensions of human experience in light of God's Word. Through their participation in the ritual actions of the liturgy, they have an opportunity to feel their own story more fully embedded within God's Story. By their very presence, they offer one another a witness to the centrality of this Story and a deepened sense of shared belonging within it.

Additionally, formal and informal school gatherings provide significant opportunities for students to process their experiences in their classes, liturgical engagements, ministry internships, and service opportunities. They need and deserve to reflect deeply on all these aspects of their education, seeking insight and integration rooted in their faith and sense of call. Through such engagements, students both contribute to and draw strength from various expressions of the Body of Christ. Such opportunities to experience community rooted in faith will certainly contribute to our students' resilience, offering hope and sustenance for their future lives so that they might thrive in the work they feel called to do.

Those of us engaged in formative theological education know that our work is both vital and complex, committed to, but encompassing much more than, a focus on important course content. As articulations of our lived faith in our particular setting, our work must intentionally foster hopeful meaning grounded in God's saving work in Christ and continuing presence among us through the Spirit. Our work must also cultivate mutually caring community as a necessary expression of our faith. In embracing these dimensions of formative theological education, we offer our students—and ourselves—the opportunity to develop the foundational cornerstone of a resilient, hopeful life stance, one grounded always in and sustained by God's love in Christ and our love for one another. When our resilience is thus connected to the very heart of Christian faith and life, we may face into the terrible headwinds of suffering, stress, and loss, hoping and trusting that these frightening realities are never our full story nor are they the end of our story. Each story—all our stories—rest within God's Story. Drawing on this ultimate meaning, we reach out in care to one another through every difficulty we will know as God holds and sustains us all.

NOTES

1. "Johns Hopkins University and Medicine Coronavirus Resource Center," Johns Hopkin's University and Medicine, https://coronavirus.jhu.edu/.

2. "Covid Hardship Watch," Center on Budget and Policy Priorities, https://www.cbpp.org/research/poverty-and-inequality/tracking-the-covid-19-economys-effects-on-food-housing-and.

3. Rebekah Levine Coley and Christopher F. Baum, "Trends in Mental Health Symptoms, Service Use, and Unmet Need for Services among U.S. Adults through the First 9 Months of the COVID-19 Pandemic," *Translational Behavioral Medicine* 11, no. 10 (October 2021): 1947.

4. Shelby Bourgault, Amber Peterman, and Megan O'Donnell, "Violence against Women and Children during COVID-19—One

Year On and 100 Papers In: A Fourth Research Round Up," *Center for Global Development Note* (April 2021): 1–10.

5. Eduardo Medina, "Mourning Families Seek Solace From the 'Grief Purgatory' of Covid-19," *New York Times*, July 31, 2021, https://www.nytimes.com/2021/07/31/us/coronavirus-grief-funerals.html.

6. Ilia Karatsoreos and Bruce McEwen, "Annual Research Review: The Neurobiology and Physiology of Resilience and Adaptation across the Life Course," Abstract, *Journal of Child Psychology and Psychiatry* 54, no. 4 (April 2013): 337.

7. Karatsoreos and McEwen, "Annual Research Review," 338.

8. Kirk Bingaman, "The Promise of Neuroplasticity for Pastoral Care and Counseling," *Pastoral Psychology* 62, no. 5 (October 2013): 550.

9. Karatsoreos and McEwen, "Annual Research Review," 343–44.

10. Karatsoreos and McEwen, "Annual Research Review," Abstract, 337.

11. Bingaman, "The Promise," 550.

12. Karatsoreos and McEwen, "Annual Research Review," Abstract, 337.

13. Steven M. Southwick and Dennis S. Charney, *Resilience: The Science of Mastering Life's Greatest Challenges*, 2nd ed. (New York: Cambridge University Press, 2018).

14. Southwick and Charney, *Resilience*, 10.

15. Southwick and Charney, *Resilience*, 16.

16. The other factors noted by Southwick and Charney as highly correlated with resilience among their research participants are "realistic optimism, facing fear, moral compass, religion and spirituality,… resilient role models, physical fitness, brain fitness, cognitive and emotional flexibility" (*Resilience*, 15–16).

17. Southwick and Charney, *Resilience*, 15.

18. Southwick and Charney, *Resilience*, 140.

19. Southwick and Charney, *Resilience*.

20. Friedrich Nietzsche, *Twilight of the Idols*, trans. Richard Polt (Indianapolis: Hackett Publishing, 1997), 6.

21. Robert Neimeyer, "Narrative Disruptions in the Construction of the Self," in *Constructions of Disorder: Meaning-Making Frameworks for Psychotherapy*, ed. Robert A. Neimeyer and Jonathan D. Raskin (Washington, DC: American Psychological Association, 2000), 207.

22. *Catechism of the Catholic Church*, 2nd ed. (Washington DC: United States Catholic Conference, 2019), §1067.

23. CCC, §1085 (italics added).

24. Southwick and Charney, *Resilience*.

25. See, for example, Greg Scott and Rachel Lovell, "The Rural Pastors Initiative: Addressing Isolation and Burnout in Rural Ministry," *Pastoral Psychology* 64, no. 1 (2015): 71–97; and Joseph Visker, Taylor Rider, and Anastasia Humphers-Ginther, "Ministry-Related Burnout and Stress Coping Mechanisms among *Assemblies of God*-Ordained Clergy in Minnesota," *Journal of Religion and Health* 56, no. 3 (June 2017): 951–61.

26. Christina Maslach, "Job Burn-Out: How People Cope," *Public Welfare*, 36 (1978): 56, quoted in Kelvin J. Randall, "Clergy Burnout: Two Different Measures," *Pastoral Psychology* 62 (2013): 334–35.

27. Dennis Shirley, "Beyond Well-being: The Quest for Wholeness and Purpose in Education," *ECNU Review of Education* 3, no. 3 (2020): 542–55. See also Dennis Shirley, "The Quest for Meaning and Purpose in Education," *Educazione: Giornale di Pedagogia Critica* 9, no. 1 (2020): 61–80.

9

CULTIVATING RELATIONALITY

Mentoring for Transformation

Theresa O'Keefe

THE PRIMARY OUTCOME of formative theological education, in any of its expressions, is to help students to listen for God's word in ever-widening contexts and peoples. Likewise, theological education is formative when it prepares students to respond in love to those contexts and peoples. Mentoring plays an essential role in reaching those outcomes, more so when it is at the service of theological education as transformative praxis.

Transformation[1]

Theological education is larger than the study of texts, ideas, practices, or communities. It is more an investigation into our dynamic relationship with the ultimate Mystery, discovered and expressed through texts, ideas, practices, and communities. From this perspective, the aim of theological education is to transform a student from a mere observer into someone who is both a shaper and a participant.

This transformative goal demands attending to two learning curves. On the one hand, formative theological education constantly calls students, and anyone else involved in this educational process, to a deeper and more expansive perspective on God and God's hope for creation. Although theological educators may be familiar with the tools of theological inquiry, they are not necessarily "experts" on God or what God desires for the world. At their best, theological educators are models, guides, and pilgrims along the way of discovery. Usually, students come to theological education in search of a deeper understanding of, relationship with, and desire to serve God. They hope to be affirmed in what they already believe and hold dear. Most students do not expect to rethink things they have never questioned. Some may be afraid of questioning what they believe. But as ongoing conversion is the work of faith, expanding perspectives is the work of theological education.

Additionally, students of theology ought to grow in awareness about how they see themselves in relationship to communities of faith. Many come to study as engaged believers and members of faith communities. Others come with a desire to serve others in light of their faith, yet they have not really considered deeply the implications and responsibilities of belonging to faith communities. Frequently students assert that churches should do this or that, with the presumption that someone else is to do it—perhaps the hierarchy or someone working at the institutional level. For too many students, church is an unquestioned, fixed, and often monolithic entity upon which they exercise little control or influence. They do not realize that they already represent the idea of church to others, and that they have a role to play in ensuring communal accountability.

Constructive-developmental theory, attending to the way humans expand their capacity to see themselves in and make meaning of their world, helps us to name the demands on a student who faces these learning curves.[2] Transformative development happens when someone, first, is able to recognize greater complexity in their world, and, second, to make better sense of what they see.[3] What has been understood previously is not lost but rather seen now within a wider ambit and reoriented in light of an expanded perspective. Viewed through the constructive-developmental lens, these two learning curves—students seeing themselves in relationship with God and in relationship to their faith community—involve just such transformation. Through a transformative learning process, students are able to come to recognize that theological perspectives have the potential to orient their lives and lend meaning, and that they themselves have distinctive roles in their relationships with God and their faith community. Faculty mentors play an essential role in helping students to understand better their particular perspectives and to recognize the richness of putting these perspectives in dialogue with theology.

Sharon Daloz Parks observes that transformation is not just a change in *how* someone thinks, but also often a change in *where* one places trust. Mentors who are trustworthy to the student have a rich role to play in their continuing growth and transformation. Parks notes, "Mentors appear when a person is discovering critical thought and must begin to take greater responsibility for both oneself and others. Mentors give you confidence that you will make it through this transition."[4] To gain a better sense of how faculty members can help students in this process in the context of formative theological education, I propose a two-step movement in a transformative process.[5]

Recognizing Transformation

Many students—graduate and undergraduate—enter theological education with conceptions of God and church that are tacit and somewhat monolithic, often presumed to be set by reliable authorities outside themselves. It is normal that a starting point for students is to assume that "we all know what we mean" when someone says "I believe in God." It rarely occurs to them to wonder *what* about God they or others believe, and *why*. This often is the case when students think about the *why* of their church affiliation as well.

A first transformative step is a conscious choice regarding one's conception of God and one's decision to be part of a faith community, something I call "self-affiliating." Students make a conscious decision about who they believe God to be and what it means to be a member of a faith community. An indication of this developmental shift is a student's ability to see their belief and their affiliation as distinct among other options, when previously belief and affiliation were unreflective and tacit. As a student sees a greater variety of options for belief or belonging among people and communities, such options are seen as value laden: students, in this more reflective posture, begin to recognize that it matters what you believe and to what group you belong.[6] With their selection comes a confidence that they have made the only right choice, or at least the best choice in the present—not only for themselves but possibly for others, too. If asked why this is the right choice, students will usually point to a trustworthy authority outside themselves, whether a sacred text, someone in church leadership, or a guide who brought them to this point.

It is helpful for theological educators to realize that students are usually brought through this transformation because they are compelled by the example of others. Faculty can help students see that belief matters for how people see themselves and engage in the world. Furthermore, they can expose students to compelling communities or persons with whom they can identify. Here, the "authority" of a compelling community, person or, yes indeed, a faculty mentor can serve as valuable models for students to orient their own lives.

Anyone who has experienced this first transformation can become a strong leader or spokesperson for a community. They can become articulate and compelling about their stance, what it means and why it is important. Likewise, they are frequently enthusiastic about being part of something bigger than themselves. There is often deep affection for and loyalty to the community chosen, and rejoicing in having found a place of belonging. In my experience, this is the stage when most graduate students enter theological education.

While there are many strengths to this first step, there are also some limitations. Chief among them is a likely inability to appreciate diversity in theological and religious expression within the faith community chosen. Students at this point tend to look at their allegiances through a binary lens, thinking that either one believes in God in the right way or one does not. When students are deeply embedded in their own choices, they are often reluctant to learn about others, usually perceived as less than or even deviant and unworthy of study. This attitude can be particularly problematic for those considering leadership positions, as they will be held responsible for and to people who may hold different perspectives. More problematic is when students assume that sustaining membership in the community of their choice requires them to deny or dismiss parts of themselves on matters such as race, gender, or sexuality in order to remain in good standing. Although this first transformative step is a major step forward in their process of self-awareness, they still need to learn to discern God's presence and action in perspectives beyond what they have come to know.

The second transformative step involves the student recognizing the tremendous diversity of perspectives in how people experience God and the church, and how such diversity is valid and enriching, not threatening. Learning about this diversity within the community can be jarring for students who assume we all believe the same thing in the same way if we are members of the same community. Mentors can accompany students in transitioning to this second step by helping them recognize how context and experience shape people's perspectives. As they hear and investigate stories of difference, especially from those they respect, they can come to see the valid diversity within the community. They can discover commonalities across diversity. What once seemed misguided, may now be recognized as a valid encounter with God, yet experienced differently. Diversity is an essential mark of every community, and at this stage students are able to see it and affirm it while taking ownership of their own perspective amidst this diversity.

In this second transformative step, students develop what Parks and Kegan call a "self-authoring" capacity. They knowingly begin to choose who and how they will be in their relationships with God and the church. Students continue to recognize the importance and influence of external voices, and their claims to authority, although do so considering the validity and richness of various other positions. They gain a transformed capacity for leadership, which allows them to listen to and weigh perspectives different from their own.

Mentors should recognize that this shift can feel risky for the student for a few reasons. First, recognizing the validity of diversity can seem like a step out of certainty. Second, while they may see themselves as distinct within the group, and thus sense some freedom in that awareness, they may also fear appearing unfaithful to the community that nurtured them up to a certain point or being at odds with others whom they love. They may worry about being judged as unorthodox. Mentors can help in at least three ways. One, be mindful of such fears. Two, help students to appreciate the many expressions of diversity within the community. Three, affirm the student's particular perspective and contribution.

Mentoring for Transformation

Mentoring is more than befriending students. It is about being appropriately transparent as we theologize and educate theologically. Transparency helps the students see the "inner workings" of the theological endeavor, demonstrating the vulnerable knowing and not-knowing the ultimate Mystery. Parks writes, "There is a gift of self on the part of the mentor, an intent and response on the part of the protégé, and a vulnerability experienced (though differently) by both."[7] Parks notes that sometimes mentors have "no awareness that their life is being watched and 'speaking volumes.'"[8] Theological educators serve as mentors simply because they stand before their students, providing access to the richness of the Christian theological tradition in a persuasive way. When theological educators are self-aware that their lives, teaching, and scholarship show students the seriousness and impact of the theological endeavor, it can help them to be intentional about how they do their own work.

If we agree that mentoring is a gift of self-offering, then we can embrace Parks's suggestion that such a gift "become[s] significant only if [it] 'makes sense' in terms of the [protégé's] own experience."[9] Therefore, theological educators as mentors should not expect every student to be similarly receptive to mentoring. They should hold this role lightly as a gift offered but not always taken.

When theological educators are not intentional about mentoring, they risk tending mainly to those who are like them and think like them, perhaps seeing something of themselves in younger colleagues. Not surprisingly, men tend to mentor men; women tend to mentor women. Such natural mentoring pattern has at least two implications. One, those accessing leadership opportunities are the ones who mirror the characteristics of their mentors. Two, the burden for mentoring nondominant students falls on the shoulders of nondominant mentors. The end result is a set of unbalanced faculty-to-student ratios among members of nondominant groups[10] and the ordeal of nondominant mentors experiencing similar exclusions (i.e., racism, sexism, or homophobia) and exhausting microaggressions, just like students from nondominant groups do. Everyone involved in theological education has an obligation to be intentionally attentive to the mentoring needs of nondominant students. We cannot assume that such needs are always met by mentors who are like them.

Willie James Jennings, in *After Whiteness: An Education in Belonging*, reflects about the challenges nondominant students face in predominant systems and cultures of theological education in the United States. He argues that theological education has been designed for a "distortion in formation." Jennings claims that theological education has been central to building up and sustaining the dominance of the "white self-sufficient man, his self-sufficiency defined by possession, control, and mastery" and "white hegemony and homogeneity."[11] All these are rooted in Western colonialism.

Jennings's strong, yet valid critique demands our attention. Not all instances of theological education may embody such colonial practices in the same way, yet most spring from a history shaped by colonization that requires intentional questioning. Christianity in the United States, by and large, has been shaped by a predominant cultural vision of the good, the right and the true rooted in European colonial principles. Tactics of removal and enslavement among Christian settlers were justified by theological doctrines that denied the full and equal humanity of entire—nonwhite—communities. Subsequently, similar theological arguments were used to justify the exclusion of Asian and Latinx communities. Theological education failed to call into question those realities. In some cases, it perpetuated them by passing them on to the next generations of Christian leaders.

In recent decades, the number of students from nondominant communities—Indigenous, Black, Latinx, Asian—and sexual and gender minorities has increased significantly in spaces of theological education in the United States. They all are heirs of a history marked by conflict and exclusion. They all are being educated, along with their white peers, in institutions that, directly or indirectly, perpetuated forms of injustice. The transformation needed in theological education in light of these realities will not come from simply replacing one perspective with another, but from considering all standpoints in light of God's expansive and healing love. Just as students of theology engage in processes of transformation triggered by the challenging of assumptions and the embrace of diverse perspectives, I as a white educator, also need to check my own assumptions and consider new perspectives. I do this largely by listening to my own students' voices and lives, and that happens through the practice of mentoring as a relationship of mutuality. I conclude describing five modalities through which such mentoring occurs.

Modes of Mentoring[12]

Mentoring at its core is about entering in relationship. Even though the relationship may not be one of equals, mutuality is expected as all involved have opportunities to grow their theological vision and agency by learning from one another. This is especially true when an environment is created wherein all are attentive to learning how to see God and the world through the eyes of another. I suggest five modes of mentoring shaping the relationship between theological educator and student. However, such relationship can also be cultivated among students so as to create a mentoring community among all.[13] I describe these modes as forms of "seeing" to suggest that mentoring helps to expand one's vision.

SEEING

Seeing refers to the faculty mentor coming to understand the student. This first step of mentoring is also perhaps the most obvious. By paying sufficient attention to students, faculty come to see them for themselves. Students' perspectives and voices are different from those of the faculty—despite likely commonalities—and require effort to recognize and acknowledge. This is increasingly true as student populations become more diverse.

Though simple and obvious, this first step unfortunately may get undercut by other obligations the mentor may have. Jennings characterizes the theological academy as a place where colonialism has limited and policed our seeing so we lose the "desire to pay attention, constant full attention to one another."[14] He describes colonialist theological education as a "superintending design" that "aims to teach [faculty as well as students] what to see and what to ignore, especially in ourselves."[15] By narrowing attention, faculty are trained to look for certain qualities or achievements in their students, and not look at the student as a full person. Jennings writes that students "lose because many of their teachers have lost attention, shed it in the heat of a formation that narrowed the intellectual excellence down to one kind of performance, one kind of white body-mind."[16]

To be authentically formative, theological education needs to resist that narrowing focus. If the hope for students is to see God more expansively in and through their encounter with others, the theological educator must take the time and effort to see students more expansively, and encourage them to do likewise. In my courses, I make the effort to help students to know one another sufficiently to be mutually helpful. This does not mean that everyone has to know everyone else equally well, yet everyone should find themselves being known well by others. This can be accomplished through conversation. Shared assignments that invite students to bring their lives in dialogue with course content helps faculty and other students learn about one another, their ways of thinking, and how they engage theological sources.

When a student comes from a very different context or seems resistant to engaging in ways that for us may be expected or more familiar, it can be challenging to understand the student's perspective. In such situations, it is essential that the theological educator makes an even greater effort to know the student. In those moments of exchange, I often remind myself to suspend judgement about the student and what they are saying so that I might really hear and understand them. If I don't do this, my prejudgment impairs my ability to understand the student on the student's own terms.[17] If I present myself as an honest broker, students are more likely to recognize that I am earnest in gaining a better understanding of them. In response, students become more forthright in their efforts to be understood. Feeling understood, whether by faculty or another student, is essential for a student to see the class and the faculty as trustworthy and thus be open to transformative learning.

SEEING WITH

Seeing *with* refers to the mentor's understanding the students' perspectives about the world. As if standing alongside them, seeing *with* considers their concerns, concepts, or communities that they are looking. By seeing *with*, the faculty mentor comes to learn what the student sees, as the student sees it, learning what the student holds dear and why. Learning to *see with* them is particularly important when students come from contexts and experiences very different from those of the mentor and other students. Apart from enabling the mentor to appreciate the unique perspectives and experiences that students bring to theological education, seeing *with* enables the mentor to reflect back to the students what is particular and valuable about their perspectives and experiences, and how those intersect with the theological endeavor.

As members of an academic community, especially one that may reflect the limitations identified by Jennings, mentors may not always recognize when theological education may be working against the students' best efforts. It can happen that students espouse ideas, concerns, or people the theological world has worked assiduously to ignore or deny. As a result of seeing *with* students, faculty can learn the validity of student concerns and expand the theological discussion in their courses and conversations. Seeing *with* may help the faculty to recognize God and God's grace in the world better as well as recognize and appreciate how and where that grace is thwarted by sinful structures. In the exercise of seeing *with*, the mentor's vision is expanded.

SEEING BEYOND

Seeing *beyond* refers to how outside perspectives can be brought into play to expand the student's seeing. Doing this is rather natural to most faculty. Yet, the goal is not to replace the student's perspective with that of the expert's, but to put them in conversation. Faculty mentors help make connections and widen the students' perspectives through critical conversation with new sources and viewpoints. Without dismissing or denying their own experience, students can come to see that different theological perspectives matter.

In light of the first level of transformation named above (i.e., self-affiliating), this means connecting theological discourse in a manner that is meaningful to the lives of the students. In light of the second level of transformation (i.e., self-authoring), the mentor can help students see how their particular perspectives inform how they engage with theological discourse and contribute to valid diversity within theological endeavors.

SEEING FOR

Seeing *for* refers to the mentor helping the student to see on behalf of others. As mentioned earlier, formative theological education is meant to have an impact upon the communities the students will serve or join. Regardless of the reasons a student engages in theological education, when they receive their credentials (e.g., graduation, ordination) people will expect much of them, and the student should be prepared for that expectation. Mentors should have a vision for the communities that the student will encounter, particularly those that give life to people with different histories, races, genders, or cultural traditions. The goal is to help students distinguish their seeing from other perspectives while discovering the impact and gift of their own perspectives.

A mentor might help students recognize the impact of their theological or ministerial choices. Frequently students presume that they are making "the right choice" following something determined beyond themselves, either by God or a church. It can be difficult for them to see their commitments as choices, rather than as predetermined blueprints. The mentor can help them see that there may be multiple choices in a given situation simply by illustrating how others have made different choices in similar situations. Alternatively, students may worry that their choices are aberrant because they differ from others. In this case, the theological educator as mentor might help them value their difference while also noting important points of connection with others. A mentor might guide students to weigh upon the likely consequences—good and bad—of their choices in the lives of others. All these strategies can help students recognize that they are making choices, and not simply following inevitabilities, even if what they do may be presented to them as normative.

BEING AWARE OF WHAT WE DO NOT SEE

Finally, *being aware of what we do not see* points to the limitations or blind spots on the part of the mentor. Even the best mentors have limitations, which can interfere with a student's growth. One blind spot can be a mentor's failure to recognize that a student is moving beyond them or moving in a direction different from what the mentor expected or hoped. Every human being sees and experiences the world differently, and mentors should not expect otherwise regarding their students. Sometimes out of caution or misplaced goodwill, mentors encourage students to conform to acceptable norms. This can be end up being harmful to students, discouraging them from bringing their whole, particular embodied lives into their theological work. More so if the lives and bodies of the students fall outside the privileged modes of existence such as being white, male, and heterosexual. Willie James Jennings writes, "This was not the kind of work that anyone should need to do."[18] Jennings's concern is not only for the individual student, but also for the communities the student represents and serves. These full lives need to be part of the theological discourse and ministerial vision. In this case, mentoring can be an act of humility in which the theological educator looks to the student for direction on how this person might be of service as a mentor. Even the best mentors will be surpassed by their mentees, many doing work that is beyond the mentor's imagination. That may be the best indication of good mentoring.

Mentors play an essential role in fostering formative theological education. They help students transform how they understand themselves, the world, and God. They do this by helping students see themselves more clearly and value their perspective while recognizing the particularity and value of other perspectives. They educate to help students develop an ever-expansive vision of God's loving work in the world.

NOTES

1. The use of transformative education in this chapter is informed by educational theorist Jack Mezirow. See particularly his *Transformative Dimensions of Adult Learning* (San Francisco: Jossey-Bass, 1991).

2. See esp. Robert Kegan, *The Evolving Self: Problem and Process in Human Development* (Cambridge, MA: Harvard University Press, 1982); and *In Over Our Heads: The Mental Demands of Modern Life* (Cambridge, MA: Harvard University Press, 1994). See also Sharon Daloz Parks, *Big Questions, Worthy Dreams: Mentoring Emerging Adults in Their Search for Meaning, Purpose, and Faith* (Minneapolis: Fortress Press, 2019); and James W. Fowler *Stages of Faith: The Psychology of Human Development and the Quest for Meaning* (San Francisco: Harper & Row, 1981).

3. Jack Mezirow argues that a transformed perspective is not simply "better" than the prior. It orders reality in a "more satisfying" way for the knower.

4. Parks, *Big Questions*, 179.

5. See Parks, *Big Questions*, 132. Note that Parks advanced her work in close conversation with Robert Kegan and James Fowler, establishing helpful connections among their respective theories.

6. Choosing against belief in God or ecclesial affiliation also fits this developmental step. To not believe or join remains an act of self-selecting.

7. Parks, *Big Questions*, 178–79.

8. Parks, *Big Questions*, 184.

9. Parks, *Big Questions*, 182.

10. During the academic year 2020–2021, the student/faculty ratio in U.S. schools accredited by the Association of Theological Schools (ATS) according to race and gender was the following: 22:1 among white faculty and students; 27:1 ratio among Black faculty and students; 24:1 among male faculty and students; 38:1 among female faculty and students. See ATS Data Tables, 2020–2021 (Pittsburgh, PA: Association of Theological Schools, 2021), https://www.ats.edu/files/galleries/2020-2021_Annual_Data_Tables.pdf pdf.

11. Willie James Jennings, *After Whiteness: An Education in Belonging* (Grand Rapids, MI: Eerdmans, 2020), 6.

12. Sharon Daloz Parks identifies five key gifts mentors offer: recognition, support, challenge, inspiration, and their own finitude, which she calls "clay feet." See Parks, *Big Questions*, 179. These five gifts inspire my reflections in this section.

13. Parks proposes higher education as a prime context for mentoring communities. See Parks, *Big Questions*, ch. 9.

14. Jennings, *After Whiteness*, 51.

15. Jennings, *After Whiteness*, 50.

16. Jennings, *After Whiteness*, 56.

17. Hans Georg Gadamer insightfully recognizes that all understanding begins in misunderstanding. See Gadamer's *Truth and Method* (New York: Continuum, 1999).

18. Jennings, *After Whiteness*, 71.

10

A PRACTICE OF FREEDOM

Imagination in Theological Education

L. Callid Keefe-Perry

> Education either functions as an instrument which is used to facilitate integration...into the logic of the present system and bring about conformity or it becomes the practice of freedom, the means by which men and women deal critically and creatively with reality and discover how to participate in the transformation of their world.[1]
>
> —Richard Shaull

ALL EDUCATION EITHER shapes us to better fit into the present order or encourages us to transform the current conditions into ones that are more just. There is no neutrally formative education. All education is formative and theological education especially so. Taken this way, the Formative Education movement is not novel because it is formative, but because (a) it is self-reflectively intending to be that way and (b) it advocates for a particular kind of formation that emphasizes specific pro-social qualities that deepen relational skills and care for the common good.[2] These are qualities that theological education ought to exemplify as well.

As I use it, the phrase "formative education" denotes a particular Jesuit-influenced quality of instruction and refers also to overlapping sets of pedagogical movements concerned with learning and "the whole person."[3] Stanton Wortham writes that when education is formative it provides opportunities in which "people become more integrated human beings who create purposeful lives together with others."[4] This is not only resonant with the goals of theological education, but *integral* to them. The task of theological education is to help students become self-reflective and fluent in the language of faith, encouraging them to explore new faithful ways of seeing and being in the world, and providing a context in which they can try on ideas that are new to them. One of the consequences of these goals is that theological education is inherently a type of formative education. Theological education must be formative to be successful.

The question is not whether theological education is formative or not, but what vision of the world is being reinforced and formed by the educational experiences being crafted. Does theological education facilitate student integration "into the logic of the present system," or does it denounce the injustices of the world and actively announce that transformation is possible? When encouraging our students to explore the faithful "practice of freedom" we also need to consider what it means for our students to "deal critically and creatively with reality." As educators concerned about the whole student and the common good, we benefit from speaking with clarity about what norms and values we are trying to free ourselves from and what future we are longing to see. One of the shifts that would be supportive of deepening the formative qualities of theological education is greater attention paid to the role of imagination in the life of faith. Below, I will show why it is that imagination can be a fruitful site for theological reflection, followed by a consideration of the ways in which this might inform pedagogy.

Imagination in Scripture

A thorough search of the NRSV Bible will reveal only four canonical references to imagination with another three found in the apocrypha.[5] The references themselves are not generally positive. For example, Ezekiel is told to "prophesy against the prophets of Israel who are prophesying" because they "prophesy out of their own imagination" (Ezek

13:2). We also get a firm reminder from Paul that "we ought not to think" that our concept of God can ever be captured as "an image formed by the art and imagination of mortals" (Acts 17:29). In both of these examples, the idea is functionally that imagination itself is a falsehood, the origin of falsehoods, or, if not outrightly false, at least not as accurate as we might want it to be. In all these cases, imagination is not something that should be referenced if one is hoping to be faithful.

If one stops there, just searching for instances of the word *imagination* in a contemporary translation of the Bible, that is the end of the road. However, there are several ways in which imagination seems to appear in the text even if it is not named explicitly. One of the dynamics that causes this to be the case has to do with the Hebrew word לֵב (*leb*), or "heart." Within the Israelite view of the human being, the heart was the home of both cognitive and emotional responses.[6] Feeling and thinking were *both* seated in the heart. One of the things that this suggests is that whenever we read about the heart in the Bible, especially if the speaker was Jewish, something more than just an emotion is going on. Consider Jesus's description of why he uses parables in Matthew 13:14–17:

> With them indeed is fulfilled the prophecy of Isaiah that says:
>
> You will indeed listen, but never understand,
> and you will indeed look, but never perceive.
> For this people's heart has grown dull,
> and their ears are hard of hearing,
> and they have shut their eyes;
> so that they might not look with their eyes,
> and listen with their ears,
> and understand with their heart and turn—
> and I would heal them.
>
> But blessed are your eyes, for they see, and your ears, for they hear. Truly I tell you, many prophets and righteous people longed to see what you see, but did not see it, and to hear what you hear, but did not hear it.

The healing of the people requires that they "understand with their heart," something they are not ready to do at least partly because their hearts have "grown dull." Something other than just sensory perception is going on here.

It is not that "many prophets and righteous people" had physical challenges with their eyes and ears. Some other issue was preventing them from perceiving what was happening: they were not yet able to imagine what Jesus was coming to preach. Once we know that it is very likely Jews would have spoken as though the heart and mind were both involved in thinking and feeling, there are several other passages that seem to look as if they might involve what we would today call "the imagination." Consider, for example, the story of the prophet Nathan and King David in 2 Samuel 12.[7]

In that passage, Nathan is headed to David to speak to the king about his abuse of power, killing Uriah the Hittite and taking his wife for his own. Rather than lead with an argument about what a king's duty ought to be, how clear the commandments are, and the ethical problems with murder and adultery, Nathan takes a different approach. He tells a story about a rich man who steals from a poor man. Nathan was apparently quite a good storyteller because we read that after hearing the story, "David's anger was greatly kindled" and he said that "as the LORD lives, the man who has done this deserves to die" (2 Sam 12:5). At this point, Nathan pivots and essentially reveals that the story was an extended metaphor, exclaiming to David, "You are the man!" This revelation and Nathan's follow-up prophesying apparently work well, because rather than defend himself or have Nathan killed, David admits that he has sinned (2 Sam 12:5). Nathan was able to get David to see something about himself that was true by first telling a story that was not.

Whenever we are asked to understand something metaphorically, we are inherently being told to hold the knowledge in a way that transcends the literal and requires us to presume something that is not the case *as if* it were. We understand that there is a metaphorical comparison going on when God is called a potter and faithful people clay (Isa 64:8) or when Jesus says that he is "the vine" and the disciples "the branches" (John 15:5). We are not supposed to take those lines to communicate that somehow God is actually a person into ceramics or that Jesus can become a plant. We recognize that this metaphorical language is being used to communicate that some qualities of potter-ness and vine-ness are also qualities of God and Jesus. This capacity for metaphorical thought entails being able to recognize that, even in considering something that is not strictly true on an empirical level (Jesus is not, in fact, a plant), there can nonetheless be truth in it.

Theologians have written powerfully about the importance of metaphor for decades,[8] and that ongoing conversation is vital and constructive. However, operating *underneath* our use of metaphor is the capacity to imagine, which undergirds our ability to interpret, produce new models, and see intimations of the new thing into which God is inviting us. Turning greater attention to what the imagination is will make it more clear how it could be more emphasized in theological education in such a way to more deeply develop qualities of positive formation.

The Generative Imagination

First, it is worth clarifying that there are different ways of categorizing imagination. As William James aptly put it, "there are imaginations, not 'The Imagination.'"[9] For example, philosophers writing in German have long differentiated between *Phantasie* and *Einbildungskraft*, or "fantasy-prone imagination" and "reality-prone imagination."[10] That is, there is a difference between the kind of imagination that layers over our actual experience with a mental veneer of more-preferred perceptions and the kind of imagination that envisions and enables possibilities which have not been considered before.

The technical distinctions articulated within a robust philosophy of imagination are not as vital to detail here as are some of their implications. Most important among these is the claim that insofar as "reality" refers to the present material conditions in which we are embedded, imagination has the capacity both to distract us from that reality *and* to help us envision a means of transforming that reality. Richard Kearney, a philosopher of religion, writes compellingly on the capacities of the creative imagination:

> The metaphors, symbols or narratives produced by imagination all provide us with "imaginative variations" of the world, thereby offering us the freedom to conceive of the world in other ways and to undertake forms of action which

> might lead to its transformation....The possible worlds of imagination can be made real by action.[11]

Were imagination just "fantasy-prone" and unable to be anything but a wallpapering over the world, it would be strange to consider it as beneficial. However, understood as also possessing "reality-prone" characteristics, the imagination is part of the way in which students can develop into "full agents who are able to enact justice and contribute to the common good of humanity."[12] Developing capacities of the generative imagination allows for the possibility of seeing new ways of being that have not yet come to be. It is part of how we "discover how to participate in the transformation" of the world.

As Jesuit John W. O'Malley writes, "inventiveness and innovation require intelligence, but beyond intelligence they entail imagination, that is, the mental agility to make a leap beyond the accepted paradigm to another and to see the relationship between them that has escaped others."[13] In this form, imagination carries with it the capacity to conceive and reconceive of possibility. Ultimately, imagination might not only enable one to conceive of new possibilities, but, brought into creative action, can birth new ways of being.[14]

Imagination is what allows us to "weep with those who weep" (Rom 12:15) even when we ourselves have not lost what has caused the tears. This is how we come to derive meaning from Jesus as the vine: we are able to hold onto descriptions of the present that are not true but reveal truth. This is reality-prone imagination in that it helps us to be empathetic and communicate complexities to others across difference. We act and are different in the world because we can imagine what it is like as another person. Imagination in the creative sense is a profoundly hermeneutic practice, shaped by an individual's mind and also by the received images and stories inherited from family, faith, and history. Consequently, conversation involving imagination necessarily entails intersubjective tendrils. Individual dreams live on, braided into generations of images, stories, legends, and hopes. The world envisioned through the creative imagination is an opening into what might yet be that takes root in the present.

Given the above, to the extent that intentionally formative theological education is concerned with "care of the whole person," I suggest that it would benefit from consideration of imaginative capacities. Imagination contributes not only to a reconsideration of present conditions and one's own sense of self, but also to the emergence of future possibilities for both of those things. The site of change in theological education is not limited to the present person and their skills, affects, knowledge, and purpose: it can also shape what it is that a person can imagine to be possible in the future for themselves and for the world. Imagination in this sense is a braided capacity, formed of strands comprised of skill, affect, and knowledge along with individual intent and cultural inheritance.

Toward an Imaginative Emphasis in Theological Education

The essay "Formative Education Online" does an excellent job of discussing formative education in the COVID-19 pandemic circumstances and a marked increase in digital-based learning.[15] Part of what the authors uncovered in their research was that more than half of the faculty members surveyed "incorporated creative assignments into their instruction," and that the assignments "gave students opportunities to unpack their feelings and the trauma that some experienced."[16] The authors of that essay reason that assessments that allowed for some creative and artistic expression "provided students with creative platforms to reflect on experiences, express vulnerability, and untangle complex emotions."[17] This is to be commended.

What is important to recognize here is that the use of "creative assignments" was specifically included for the purposes of allowing for greater affective communication and the processing of experience. This use of "creative assignments" seems effective and apt because "using art" has been *integrated* into the lesson and is not just tacked on as an afterthought. Use of the arts does not automatically shift one's pedagogy to become intentionally formative: attention must be given to considering how it is that the arts might communicate in registers that are broader than what would likely come through traditional academic assessment. Given the commitments of formative education across content, context, and character, the use of creative assignments seems fitting. However, the resonances with imagination run even deeper still, especially in formative *theological* education.

In much of the literature that takes up questions of how religion or spirituality intersect with creativity, imagination, and art, there is often a kind of overly simplistic accounting that is done. Religion and spirituality that uses the arts and communicates in creative, imaginative, and aesthetic ways is good and in touch with life-giving parts of tradition. Theological thinking that uses "regular" means of communication—academic prose, traditional sermon styles, no attempts to engage visual media, and so on—is bad, or, at least outmoded. I myself have been guilty of this kind of reductive assessment in the past, so I understand its appeal. What I have come to believe, however, is that while there is ample reason to be excited about the consideration of imagination in religious reflection, the reality of the situation is more complex than a simple division of "theology with imagination" and "theology without imagination."

Associating the imagination mostly with "creativity" or "the arts" obscures the fact that our imaginations are *always* employed whenever we are thinking about the world around us, how we might act in it, and what it means that God is active in our lives. Compellingly, the connection between imagination and formation is not only theoretically interesting but has empirical evidence as well. Religious education scholar David Loomis has published a psychological study with some encouraging findings suggesting that imagination might be worth giving greater attention to in theological education.

First, Loomis finds that there is a strong positive association between increased capacity for "imaginative insight" and religious maturity. Second, that an individual's capacity for imaginative thinking has a more significant association with religious awareness than do factors such as religion in the home and whether or not someone is clergy.[18] A person's ability to imagine the world transformed seems to contribute to a positive engagement with religion. Furthermore, in a parallel to the distinction between "reality-prone" and "fantasy-prone" imagination types, the study reveals that the positive linkages to religious maturity in the "fantasy" domain are significantly less than in the "creative imagination" one.[19] Imagination is part of a life of faith even when the arts are not involved at all.

Another way of thinking about this is to say that the phrase "a lack of imagination" doesn't hold up to much scrutiny. I think that what people mean when they talk about "a lack of imagination" is that things are not changing enough for their preferences. Consider this passage from an interview with Rodger Nishioka, a Presbyterian religious education scholar:

> One of the ordination questions we ask of people in my Presbyterian tradition is, "Will you serve the people with energy, intelligence, imagination, and love?" I'm so grateful that the writers of that liturgy put the word "imagination" in there, because frankly, I'm a little worried these days that we lack a theological imagination. I think over and over again that one of the things that makes us created in the image of God, uniquely as beings on the face of the earth, is that God instills in humankind the ability to imagine...the ability to move beyond whatever the concrete limitations are of our lives and to think thoughts that take us into distant places that we may never have dreamed before. That's an imagination. And a theological imagination is one that is attentive to how God is at work in the world.[20]

I support the direction in which Nishioka is headed. However, I think it is a mistake to say that today we "lack a theological imagination."

It is more accurate to say that the current patterns of dominant theological imagination are not ones he likes as much as what might come next. The state of things theological is the *result* of dominant theological imaginations, not the absence of imagination. The way that we currently discuss God is already a function of our imagination. It is not that the options are "imagination" and "no imagination." It is that patterns of imagination wrestle with one another for our attention and we form habits and practices that maintain or disrupt ways of imagining. Just as there is no neutrally formative education, there are no imagination-less ways of engaging with the world. Education either shapes us to better fit into the present order or it encourages us to transform the current conditions to ones that are more just.

As theological educators it is part of our job to help students develop the habit of seeing God in all things. This task is more easily accomplished when we provide educational environments that encourage the cultivation of an internal freedom to explore the new ways that God is making where there has been no way. If God's ways and thoughts are indeed more than humans can fully comprehend (Isa 55:8–9), our only option is an imaginative and faithful act. As Jesuit literary scholar Robert Barth wrote, "it is only the imagination that can bring us to the full encounter with religious reality because it is only the symbolic language of imagination that can resist the human drive for simple clarity and determinateness."[21] The imagination does not provide answers but draws us into deeper consideration of what might be possible. We can never know the interior landscape of another fully: we must imagine what is in there. We act and are different in the world because we can imagine what it is like as another person. We become better connected to people and ideas, recognizing that empathy and interpretation both have their roots in imagination.

For those who are religious this same logic plays out in an exponentially magnified way when considering possibilities like "God's justice" and "peace on earth." Do I think these things are possible? I *imagine* so. Ultimately, though, I must take it on faith, developing a conviction though I have not yet seen them in their fullness. I think about what happened to Saul on the road to Damascus and how afterward he not only experienced the world differently but experienced *himself* differently in relation to it. What he imagined to be possible had radically shifted. This seems similar to theologian Garrett Green's claim that the imagination is the "point of contact" where human experience encounters revelation.[22] Creative imagining can be a generative hermeneutic act by which people bridge the gap between themselves and the unknown as it presents itself in the face of the Other and in possibility of the future.

Future Work

> Free to play with the givens, to reject or distort input, at the interface between our senses and ourselves, our imagination has a terrible power over our inner life, over the decisions we make....Educating the imagination...is thus of primordial importance.[23]
>
> —Janine Langan

Formative education explicitly gives attention to collaborative inquiry, the importance of interdisciplinary exploration, and the application of knowledge to community context and student flourishing.[24] It is also the case that it has an implicit curriculum that recognizes the importance of imagination and the consideration of how the work of learning can be yoked to creative personal reflection and transformation of self and world. This is to be commended. However, additional attention to developing creative and imaginative skills and habits could provide even greater benefits resonant with the commitments in formative education, especially in contexts of formative *theological* education.

As people of faith it is important that we recognize how important our imagination is. We ought to be concerned about the ways in which we make room for intentional reflection on it—or not—in our churches and communities. This is doubly true for those of us who are theological educators. I firmly believe that imagination is implicated "in our ability both to internalize collective habits of thought *and* to free ourselves from them."[25] Without attention to both of these functions of imagination, I fear we are not getting as full of a sense of things as we could. Our liberation and domination are tied to our ability to imagine.

As a theological educator, part of what I want to provide for my students is an environment in which they not only have the *opportunity* to imagine what transformation God might be calling forth, but one in which they are actively *encouraged* to listen for what comes next. I want to make sure that in addition to an increase of knowledge and skills my students also have an increased inclination to explore and experiment with what faithfulness might mean for them. To this end, I think that an increased emphasis on the imaginative dynamics of theological education can help to better provide conditions in which to reflect on the nature of the consequences of the stories told, the metaphors used, and the kind of world we imagine is possible. This can mean an increased use of the arts in our classrooms, but more deeply than that it ought to include reflection on both the content and method of our teaching and assessment.

In addition to helping students understand where the church has been and how we talk about the enduring questions of faith today, theological education as a space for the "practice of freedom" must make room for students to reflect on what God may be calling forth. This means that our schools need to be places in which students learn to question the "logic of the present system." This includes large questions about injustices in the world as well as inquiries at a different scale about the way classrooms and curricula are constructed. Designing our courses to be intentionally formative means we will end up with students who discover they can see beyond the horizon farther than we have: students who can imagine new forms of faithfulness and service. Perhaps they may also see new ways of assessment as well.

At a bare minimum, we might make more explicit use of a broad range of arts, considering how they could be part of instruction and assessment. More substantively we could consider if the *form* of our class design is as broad as it could be. Do our classes engage and honor embodied experience? Do we value the wisdom found in story and song? Are we trying to form the whole person or just the cognitive aspects of them? Are we teaching for the church that is coming or that church that has gone?

Educators teaching within theological education programs are beautifully positioned to lead the way in integration of more explicit engagement with the creative imagination in our curricula. In the years to come, we can explore and innovate in ways that shed light on practices that can equally benefit our students and provide examples for our peers in other departments. At least, I imagine we can.

NOTES

1. Richard Shaull, introduction to *Pedagogy of the Oppressed*, by Paulo Freire (New York: Continuum, 1990), 15.

2. This categorization is based on the work of Deoksoon Kim, Stanton Wortham, Katrina Borowiec, Drina Kei Yatsu, Samantha Ha, Stephanie Carroll, Lizhou Wang, and Julie Kim. See "Formative Education Online: Teaching the Whole Person during the Global COVID-19 Pandemic," *AERA Open* 7 (May 2021), https://journals.sagepub.com/doi/10.1177/23328584211015229.

3. John W. O'Malley, "Jesuit Schools and the Humanities: Yesterday and Today," *Studies in the Spirituality of Jesuits* 47, no.1 (2015): 1–34.

4. Stanton E. F. Wortham, "How Can We Educate Whole Human Beings?" News & Videos, Boston College Lynch School of Education and Human Development, June 25, 2018, https://www.bc.edu/bc-web/schools/lynch-school/lynch-news/2018-news-archive/how-can-we-educate-whole-human-beings.html.

5. Prov 18:11; Ezek 13:2, 17; Acts 17:29; 2 Esd 6:5; 16:54, 63.

6. For example, Prov 3:3;6:21; and 7:3 all give the heart as the center of thinking and reason, and Prov 15:15 and 15:30 have emotions there as well.

7. I'm indebted to Garrett Green for his reflection on the imagination in this passage.

8. Perhaps most famously is Sallie McFague's *Metaphorical Theology : Models of God in Religious Language* (Philadelphia: Fortress Press, 1982).

9. William James, *The Principles of Psychology*, vol. 2 (New York: Dover, 1950), 50.

10. The English translation of these concepts I take from David Loomis; the historical philosophical engagement is well documented in Richard Kearney, *Wake of Imagination: Toward a Postmodern Culture* (London: Routledge, 1998), 15.

11. Richard Kearney, *Poetics of Imagining: Modern to Postmodern* (New York: Fordham University Press, 1998), 149.

12. Kim, Wortham, et al., "Formative Education Online," 2.

13. John W. O'Malley, "Jesuit Schools and the Humanities Yesterday and Today," 28–29.

14. Paul Ricœur argues that the generative imagination is "connected with an ontology" and that the new possibilities seen via imaginative exploration lead to "a kind of second ontology" in which new ways of being enter the world first through the imagination and then later in substance and action (Ricœur, "Lectures," 19:13, quoted in George H. Taylor, "Ricœur's Philosophy of Imagination," *Journal of French and Francophone Philosophy* 16, no. 1/2 (Spring/Fall 2006): 98.

15. Kim, Wortham, et al., "Formative Education Online.

16. Kim, Wortham, et al., "Formative Education Online," 7.

17. Kim, Wortham, et al., "Formative Education Online," 7.

18. David J. Loomis, "Imagination and Faith Development," *Religious Education* 83, no. 2 (1988): 260.

19. Loomis, "Imagination and Faith Development," 260.

20. The interview itself can be seen here: Rodger Nishioka, "Bible Study that Transforms: Imagination," interview for the Yale Youth Ministry Institute, YouTube video, December 19, 2012, https://www.youtube.com/watch?v=s9_EXaFj2lc.

21. J. Robert Barth, *Romanticism and Transcendence: Wordsworth, Coleridge, and the Religious Imagination* (Columbia: University of Missouri Press, 2003), 7.

22. Garrett Green, *Imagining God: Theology and the Religious Imagination* (Grand Rapids, MI: Eerdmans, 1998).

23. Janine Langan, "The Christian Imagination," in *The Christian Imagination: The Practice of Faith in Literature and Writing*, rev. and exp. ed., ed. Leland Ryken (Colorado Springs, CO: Shaw Books, 2002), 65.

24. Kim, Wortham, et al., "Formative Education Online."

25. Mark Fettes, "Senses and Sensibility: Educating the Somatic Imagination," *Journal of Curriculum Theorizing* 27, no. 2 (2011): 114–29.

CONTRIBUTORS

John F. Baldovin, SJ, is Professor of Historical and Liturgical Theology. He has a PhD from Yale and has taught at Fordham University (1981–1984), the Jesuit School of Theology at Berkeley (1984–1999), Weston Jesuit School of Theology (1999–2008), and Boston College since 2008. His interests comprise the history of the liturgy, eucharistic theology, the liturgical calendar, and the post–Vatican II liturgical reform and its critics. He is past president of the North American Academy of Liturgy and of the international ecumenical Societas Liturgica.

Andrew R. Davis is Associate Professor of Old Testament. He has written on biblical theology, biblical historiography, literary approaches to biblical narrative, ancient Israelite religion, and the Book of Job. His most recent work focuses on the Bible's prophetic literature, especially the Books of Amos and Isaiah.

Colleen M. Griffith, Faculty Director of Spirituality Studies and Professor of the Practice of Theology, teaches and writes at the intersection of theology and spirituality studies. She has research interests in theological anthropology, historical and contemporary spirituality, and method in practical theology. Her most recent publication is *Práticas espirituais católicas: Um tesouro de coisas novas e velhas* (Apostolado da Oraçao, 2022), a Portuguese translation of her coedited book *Catholic Spiritual Practices: A Treasury of Old and New* (Paraclete, 2014). Griffith's edited volume *Prophetic Witness: Catholic Women's Strategies for Reform* (Crossroad, 2009) received a 2010 first place award from the Catholic Press Association.

Thomas H. Groome is Professor of Theology and Religious Education at Boston College and long serving Director of BC's renowned PhD in

Theology and Education. Tom is the author of more than ten books and collections, of two grade school catechetical series (K to 8th grade from W. H. Sadlier), and is primary author of the Credo high school theology curriculum (from Veritas/Benziger). Tom has lectured widely throughout the United States and in more than twenty-five countries. His most recent book is *What Makes Education Catholic* (Orbis, 2021).

L. Callid Keefe-Perry is Assistant Professor of Contextual Education and Public Theology. He also serves as Assistant Director of the Religion and Education Collaborative, researching issues of religion and spirituality in public education. His scholarship engages themes of public and practical theology, critical pedagogy, and theologies of imagination. Recently, he has explored how moral injury and trauma relate to learning and spiritual formation. He is an active Quaker minister at Fresh Pond Monthly Meeting in Cambridge, Massachusetts.

Melissa M. Kelley is Associate Professor of Pastoral Care and Counseling. Her teaching and research interests include pastoral-theological and narrative perspectives on grief, loss, and resilience as well as justice-centered pastoral formation and practice. She is a pastoral psychotherapist through the Association for Clinical Pastoral Education and a Fellow in Thanatology through the Association for Death Education and Counseling. She is the author of *Grief: Contemporary Theory and the Practice of Ministry* (Fortress Press, 2010).

Richard Lennan (Dr. Theol., University of Innsbruck) is a priest of the diocese of Maitland-Newcastle (Australia). He is Professor of Systematic Theology and chair of the Ecclesiastical Faculty; his research and teaching focus on ecclesiology, ministry, and the theology of Karl Rahner. His most recent books are *Tilling the Church: Theology for an Unfinished Project* (Liturgical, 2022) and, as coeditor, *Priestly Ministry and the People of God: Hopes and Horizons* (Orbis, 2022).

Theresa O'Keefe is a Professor of the Practice in Religious Education and Youth and Young Adult Faith at Boston College School of Theology and Ministry. She is interested in how constructive-developmental psychology can inform how we minister to and educate those maturing in faith. Her book *Navigating toward Adulthood: A Theology of Ministry with Adolescents* (Paulist Press, 2018) argues that robust relationships within communities of faith are the most valuable means for young people to mature in faith.

Hosffman Ospino is Associate Professor of Theology and Religious Education and serves as Chair of the Department of Religious Education and Pastoral Ministry at Boston College School of Theology and Ministry. He studies how culture shapes theological and ministerial education. He has conducted several national studies on how Hispanic Catholics are transforming U.S. Catholicism. He has authored/edited 15 books and more than 150 essays, academic and general. He is a former president of the Academy of Catholic Hispanic Theologians of the United States (ACHTUS).

Nancy Pineda-Madrid holds the T. Marie Chilton Chair of Catholic Theology at Loyola Marymount University. She taught at Boston College from 2005 to 2019 and currently teaches during summer sessions. She does constructive work in soteriology and on theological symbols. She has published two monographs, *Theologizing in an Insurgent Key: Violence, Women, Salvation* (Paulist Press, 2022) and *Suffering and Salvation in Ciudad Juárez* (Fortress, 2011). She also coedited two volumes, one on the Holy Spirit and another one on hope.